Local Gold

BRIGETTE MANIE

ISBN-10: 1500388467
ISBN-13: 978-1500388461

Cover Design: ebookcoversgalore.com

Edited by Hazel McGhie

Printed in the United States of America by Createspace.com

DEDICATION

To every woman who crossed oceans looking for Mr. Right only to find treasure in your own backyard.

"And you *swallowed* that too." His inflection intimated that she'd gone past gullible to idiotic.

"I don't appreciate your tone, suggesting that I'm stupid!" Brianna snapped, anger lacing her words.

Bart didn't feel like tiptoeing around her tonight. He didn't feel like putting her feelings first. He had been doing that in this whole relationship, acquaintanceship, or whatever in God's name was between them. It wasn't happening tonight. "I didn't suggest a thing," he said flatly. "If you feel stupid, you did that all by yourself."

She flew from her seat, and Bart wondered if she was going to take a swing at him what with the way she balled her hands into fists and pressed them atop the table. He kind of hoped she would. His aggravation needed some sort of physical outlet, and if she took a swing at him he wasn't going to take it docilely. He wouldn't hit her back. He wasn't like that, but he wouldn't put shaking some sense into her past his capabilities tonight.

"I think you'd better leave," she declared through her teeth.

He wasn't going anywhere. "I pay seventy-five percent of the rent for this house. I think I'm entitled to sit anywhere in this building that I see fit."

"Well that's my chair and this is my dining room table so find something else to sit on!" She shouted.

"You're going to wake Jonathon up," he warned.

"I don't care. You started this."

"I didn't start anything. You brought this mess in here tonight."

TITLES BY BRIGETTE MANIE

The Banning Island Series

Against His Will

Tropical Eyewitness

Five Brothers Books

From Passion to Pleasure

Once in This Lifetime

Someone Like You

Not His Choice

Local Gold

The Seneca Mountain Romances

A Fall for Grace

A Price Too High

All Things Work Together (novella)

Mahogany and Daniel

A Man Apart

Forever With You

.

CHAPTER I

EAVESDROPPERS never hear good things about themselves.
They never hear good things period. Brianna stood outside the
door to Bart's apartment, fuming. He was buying a house and
hadn't told her—the wretch! He planned to leave her stuck
with the $1,700 monthly rent that she could not afford on her
own. Not bothering to knock, she slapped her hand on the
door and blazed in. "When were you going to tell me you were
buying a house?" she demanded, glaring at the toast brown,
curly haired man seated on the sofa, same one who'd occupied
her dream last night.

Bart looked up from the paperwork in his hands. "Hello to
you too, Brianna. Jonathon's asleep. Do you want to leave him
up here until tomorrow?"

"You didn't answer me," she reminded him, ignoring his
question.

"I planned to tell you after I was in contract. It didn't seem
to make sense saying something before since so many offers can
fall through."

"After!" she exclaimed shrilly. "You planned to abandon
me and Jonathon, and then just tell us in an after-thought, Oh,

I'm moving out guys. I bought a house."

"Keep your voice down, Bri, or you'll wake up Jonathon."

"Oh, you care about waking him up but not about leaving him without shelter?" she scoffed. "You know I can't pay the rent for this whole house by myself if you leave."

"And you know I wouldn't leave you alone to do that; so please don't accuse me falsely. I'm not buying a house for myself. I plan to take you and Jon with me."

"I'm twenty-seven years old Bart and have been on my own for some time now. If you plan something with me in mind, make sure I know about it *before* and not *after* the fact."

"What's with you tonight?" he asked, frowning at her. "Why are you picking a fight?"

"I'm not," Brianna denied. "I'm just upset that you didn't think it important to tell me that you were moving out."

"I'm not moving out!" He snapped, slapping the papers in his hands roughly unto the cushion beside him.

"So your buying a house is what?" she challenged.

He looked at her like he didn't recognize her. "What is wrong with you? Did you have a rough day at the gym? Why are you so crabby?"

"Why are you so inconsiderate?" she shot back.

"Inconsiderate!" Bart rose swiftly from the sofa and faced her head on. "I'm inconsiderate? Let's look at my record. Who picks Jon up from school most days? Who reads to him at night? Who takes him to music lessons? Who takes care of him on the Sundays that you work?" He glared at her. "What happened? Lost some steam?" he taunted when she didn't answer. "Thought you might."

Brianna wanted to kick him in his most vulnerable spot. It didn't help that his insensitivity had nothing to do with Jonathon and everything to do with her. But he didn't need to know that; so she said aloud, "I lost steam and you lost my trust. Now I have to explain to him that his dad is leaving. I'll just get my son." She moved to bypass him, headed for the bedrooms.

Bart caught her arm firmly as she tried that. "Don't you *dare* tell him any such thing," he commanded.

"Excuse me?" *Who was he talking to? It couldn't be her.* "I *am* his mother."

"And I'm his father."

Brianna's laugh came out as a husky and derisive sound. "You're only that because I say you are. Biologically you have no say so."

"How about economically?" he asked silkily.

"I never asked you to support him!" Brianna said vehemently, resisting his forward pull.

"Yet you didn't refuse that support."

"Don't throw that in my face." She gave him a killer look. "And let me go." She placed her hands against his chest and strained away from him. His hold only solidified the more she tried to break free. "What do you think you're doing?"

"Stopping you from waking up my son and telling him foolish things."

"Let me go," she demanded again.

"Not until we work through your anger and frustration. What's really bothering you?"

He knew her too well. They'd been friends for more than seven years and roommates for six. This was one time though that she couldn't tell him the fullness of her aggravation because he was at the source of it: Him and the fact that his blue eyes distracted her from her work and made her spacey in the middle of weight training—dangerous thing that; him and the fact that his touch made her pulse skitter and scatter; him and the feel of his washboard abs against her through the thin fabric of her workout shirt which made her wish he'd ditch his shirt, drop and do a hundred pushups with her beneath him as the exercise mat. Good God, she needed a mental evaluation!

"What's wrong Bri, Bri?"

Brianna sighed and fantasized them together on some tropical island, his capable hands sliding down her body and his fingers making the spreading of sunscreen an erotic exercise. She groaned and squeezed her eyes tightly shut at the direction of her thoughts.

"It's that bad, huh?" he asked, cradling her head against his shoulder and massaging tension out of her neck.

If he kept touching her like this, continued whispering in her ear, and kept making understanding sounds, Brianna knew she would tell him how much she cared for and desired him. To avoid making a fool of herself, she blamed all her frustration on the job. "My schedule was ridiculous today. Tanya was out sick, and I had to cover most of her classes. My private client was a half hour late and still wanted a full session, which I only gave because he paid me for the extra half hour along with the regular forty-five minute workout. I'm so tired that I almost fell asleep coming home. A cop stopped me and made me take a sobriety test—said he'd been following me for ten minutes and I was driving erratically! I didn't get a ticket but would you believe he tried to pick me up?" She felt him stiffen and wondered at his reaction.

"What did you do?" he asked.

With that calm question, Brianna figured she'd imagined his tension. "I told him I was married with a child and with another on the way. He almost tripped over his feet rushing to his patrol car especially when he heard that I might be in the family way." She laughed as she replayed the scene in her head.

The man almost killed himself trying to run away.

Bart chuckled at her description. "I bet he'll think twice before he hit on another woman while on duty, at least for a while."

Brianna relaxed against him, letting her exhausted body go pliant in his arms. She felt contented when he gathered her closer to his chest. It had been a rough day at the gym. Personal training wasn't the easiest business to be in.

"I can run you a bubble bath," he offered.

And this is why this guy is special. "That sounds like heaven," Brianna murmured with a lengthy exhalation.

"Okay, sit here while I fill the tub."

"I don't want to move," she protested.

"Bri, the sofa's right next to us," Bart laughed.

"I know, but I'm comfortable where I am right now." And she truly was. He was warm and smelled like earth sprinkled with rain. Brianna sucked in more of his scent. It stirred her in ways that weren't proper, but he didn't know, so no harm no foul right?

"I'll help you down," he said, tilting her backwards and easing her down unto the sofa. Brianna went but didn't release him. She ended up seated with him bent over her and with his arms braced against the back of the sofa.

"You have to let me go," he murmured, smiling at her.

"I can't. My hands are numb." She grinned at him, knowing this was more than friendly playfulness, but unable to resist flirtation.

"Soooo," he drawled, "I guess we'll stay like this?"

"That's not a bad idea."

"You won't get your bath," he pointed out.

"But I'll get...," She trailed off. *You* was what she was going to say, but she didn't want to be so obvious.

"What will you get?" The question came out in a husky rumble.

When their eyes met, his were filled with the heat of awareness, which Bri could only imagine mirrored hers. Her lips felt dry. She moistened them with her tongue. The action captured his attention. Her breath paused when his eyes fell to her mouth, and then respiring through her nose wasn't enough. Her lips parted, and she exhaled in quick puffs of air and inhaled even faster.

"I think you ought to let me go or…" His voice sounded like sandpaper rubbing on concrete.

"Or what?" Bri whispered. *You'll kiss me?* Her answer would be 'Yes, please'. She didn't find out. Gently, Bart reached up and pulled her hands from around his neck. He placed them carefully in her lap. "I'll go get your bath ready," he said, not answering her question at all. With a longing look at her mouth, he walked away to do what he promised.

CHAPTER II

If they kept this up, he'd end up losing his mind. Well his heart was already gone so what was one more organ? Bart turned on the faucets of his bathtub and watched the water gushing out of the tap and swirling into the tub. Sometimes like just now, he'd start thinking that he should say what was in his heart. The way she looked at him mere moments ago made him think that if he made a move she wouldn't mind. They flirted a lot, but it never went anywhere. One of them always called a halt to things except that one time two years ago when he'd tasted her for the first time. That kiss had been succulent and sensual, and he wanted more. But neither of them had taken things to that level again, and they hadn't spoken about it afterwards either.

Bart loosened his tie. He got heated thinking about it. Something had to give—either his sanity, but he needed that, or his reserve. He had to get over the fear that she'd reject making this friendship a partnership—the marital kind. The attraction between them was real, but it could be more. He wanted it to be more, but did she? She appeared comfortable with just flirtation, which she did a lot. He wanted the whole enchilada—wife, home, and family. Right now he had the illusion of it. His and Brianna's domestic situation was nearly marital, but not quite. Dare he reach for more?

He reached into the medicine chest and added her favorite scents, Midnight Mist and Tropical Tastebuds, to her bath water. It wasn't the first time that he'd made her a bubble bath. He kept fragrances in his bathroom for moments like this. Bart turned the faucet off.

"Brianna," he called.

She didn't answer.

He left the bathroom and found her fast asleep on the sofa, her hands neatly placed in her lap the way he'd left them and her head lolling to the side. With her face relaxed in sleep, she seemed vulnerable and in need of protection. Bart smiled at the thought, knowing that the five foot one inch woman was quite capable of taking care of herself. Fiercely independent, you'd never know if she were in pain or in need, because she'd never say. From the day he met her, three months pregnant, she'd been that way. It was something he admired about her. He'd gotten her a job as a receptionist that summer with the law firm he worked with. She'd worked hard and well. The partners had requested that she stay on part time when she returned to school. She'd held down that job until she finished school, supplementing her income with group exercise instructorships in gyms. The only time she'd been without employment was during her six week maternity leave. Only his insistence that she needed to take the full leave prevented her from returning to work earlier. Getting her to take financial support for Jonathon from him hadn't been easy. With her not having health coverage, the bills had been unmanageable. She'd reluctantly taken the help he was more than happy to give to the woman he'd privately come to love and the child he loved and claimed as his own.

Her complexion resembled the pine-colored wood of the head and foot boards of his bed—so smooth, he felt like trailing the backs of his fingers across her face. Her black eyebrows, threaded to perfectly arched lines, matched her black lashes, curled up just a whisper at the tips. Her short, slightly upturned nose seemed to pull her upper lip upright a bit, making her mouth more heart shaped and cuter than it already was. Bart could look at her forever and not get weary. She was that pretty. The ponytail had given up the struggle to hold her hair in place. Strands, curling now that the wetness of the workout had worn off, fell across her forehead and twisted on her temples in jet black ringlets. She sighed and shifted, her movement causing her workout shirt to define the evidences of her womanhood more clearly.

Bart glanced away, trying to shut down the ideas that were germinating in his head at the sight of Bri's bosom. "Bri?" He touched her arm. Her eyes fluttered open and reflected a moment of confusion before they cleared and she smiled at him.

Bart tried not to make his heart flutter as her lips curved and widened. When it started pounding he figured he'd lost the battle so why stress? "Your bath is ready," he told her.

"Thanks, Bart. I don't think I can make it to the bathroom alone though. Will you help me?"

No one had to tell him that helping her to her bath was a bad idea. He knew it just like he knew he would help her, because there wasn't much that he could refuse Brianna Robinson. "Let's take your shoes off first," he suggested, kneeling and loosening her Nike's and slipping them off with her socks.

"Now what?"

Bart heard the teasing in her voice and figured she was back to flirting mode again. He chose not to engage. His endurance had its limit. He liked to believe he was strong but was realistic enough to know he wasn't invincible. "Now I take you to the bathroom, and you can change the rest of your clothes."

"By myself?" she said plaintively.

"By yourself," he said firmly, standing and scooping her up from the sofa.

"What am I going to wear? My clothes are downstairs."

They shared a house. He lived in the upstairs apartment, and she had the first floor. "You can borrow one of my T-Shirts."

"What about under—"

"And here we are," Bart hastily interrupted her. He was not discussing underwear with her. He was also not going downstairs to riffle through her intimate garments when his libido was skyrocketing while only imagining her in them. Disaster is what he'd be inviting if he got an actual visual of what she wore beneath those yoga pants.

He flipped the toilet's cover down and seated her on it. "You take it from here," he said and turned to make a quick exit.

"What if I can't?"

The question froze him in place. Bart swallowed and answered carefully. "You're tired not incapacitated, Bri."

"What if I were?"

Nothing in her tone hinted at the motive behind that. Bart turned, hoping to find a revelation in her expression. Nothing. He couldn't get a reading on her state of mind. "What do you mean?" Was she saying that she'd want him disrobing her if she couldn't do it herself for whatever reason? His heart started knocking urgently against his ribcage.

"I think you know what I mean." The smile she sent

towards him was tinged with wryness.

Bart was about to protest that he didn't when she reached for the hem of her shirt. He swallowed his words and all but sprinted out of there. He heard Bri's low laugh as he closed the door behind him. Bart headed for the kitchen. He needed an ice cold glass of water. It was either that or a cold shower, but since she was in his bathroom, going there wasn't an option.

CHAPTER III

Dallas, Texas the next day

"F-I-R-E-D," the president for the Central South Conference of Second Advent Believers (SAB) Churches spelled the word out since he'd been asked for repetition.

Christopher stared at the man stunned. Maybe he was having an outer body experience. This wasn't happening to him. He was too good, too much of an asset, and too dynamic a preacher for them to fire him. They needed him. He shot to his feet, the humility he'd cultivated over the years caving in to injured and outraged pride. "You can't do this. I'm the best preacher you've got. I've raised up three congregations for this conference and grown two from missions to two hundred plus church memberships. In addition I—"

"Sit down and be quiet!" President Washington interrupted him sharply. "I know all that you've done. That's not why I'm firing you. You're a good preacher, Chris, but your lifestyle has to witness as well as your words. Your affair with Shayla Thompson is one of the things that got you fired."

"I told you that her accusations were that of a scorned woman," Christopher protested as he regained his seat.

"Well it seems not. We have evidence of the affair."

Christopher's heart lurched. "Evidence?"

"Yes. We have a recording with you and her…together." The man cleared his throat in discomfort.

"An audio?" he asked, his mind frantically working to see how to extricate himself from this mess.

"Yes."

"If it's an audio, how do you know the voice is mine?"

President Washington shook his head wearily. "You can't get out of this one, son. She called your name and you responded."

"That's on the recording?" Christopher made his voice skeptical but could hear the final nail being hammered into his coffin.

The president held up an RCA voice recorder. "Shall I play it?"

"No," Christopher said dully, his shoulders slumping in defeat. He knew what he would hear—his guilt coming back to haunt him. Men shouldn't be deceived, for they will reap what they sow because God can't be mocked. The admonition of the Scriptures in Galatians 6:7 echoed in his head. He'd sown seeds of fornication for too long, perverting the word of God and casting shadows over Christianity in the eyes of those who knew of his indiscretions. But God, who could not be mocked, had enough and allowed him to be exposed.

"You were a bright star, Christopher, the brightest in this conference; but instead of letting your light shine for Christ, you've covered it with a crimson life of sinfulness. Now we have no choice but to release you." Moses Washington shook his head again, sadness in the gesture and his expression this time. "I said this is one of the things that led to your dismissal. It's not the only thing."

Christopher got tense in his seat. What else did his boss—former boss—have on him?

"I know about Mirlande Stevens."

What did he know about her?

"I know that she planned to leave her husband to be with you, but you didn't want her. I also know that the child she has and which her husband claims is yours."

"You can't prove any of that," Christopher objected, some of his natural cockiness coming out now that the soil wasn't shifting beneath him so much.

"DNA test on the child could prove it, but neither Mirlande nor her husband is willing to have it done. She confessed to me in her husband's presence. Later she withdrew the confession, and he denied she'd made it. I couldn't take it further and confront you, but you've been under scrutiny since then."

"Mirlande Stevens was lying," Christopher maintained, confident now that the truth of that sin couldn't be verified.

"So were Brianna Robinson seven years ago and Selena Myers before that."

Christopher jerked in his seat, belying his guilt.

"You didn't know I knew about them, did you?"

Wisdom prevailed and he kept silent.

"Seven years ago when you came to this conference for employment," Moses Washington continued, "I only hired you because of my friendship with your father. Back then you were considered leprous. Nobody wanted to touch you. Gaylor Potts, the president from Mid-America Conference who withdrew your employment offer due to your involvement with Brianna Robinson, personally called me to tell me not to give you a job. Apparently her family had influence with him."

Witch! Christopher seethed. He'd always suspected that she robbed him of that coveted pastoral opportunity to lead the largest congregation in Mid-America at the Patmos SAB Church. Now he knew for sure that she'd blocked his way.

"I hired you despite the cloud hanging over your head. No other conference president would have picked you up then or given you the opportunity I did. I'd hoped that you would have reformed and forsaken your old ways. Instead, since then you've compromised yourself and the gospel twice. I cannot help you this time Christopher, not with what's on this." He held up the recording device again.

Pushing back his chair, he stood. "On your way out, stop by Payroll. I've instructed them to cut your final check. It will include any sick and vacation days you've accrued." President Washington walked around the desk and stopped in front of Christopher.

Christopher stood up, not wanting to feel overwhelmed by the man's height.

"Let me have your ministerial credentials, Christopher." He extended his hand for the ID card that identified Christopher as an ordained minister of the SAB church.

Christopher's hand shook as he withdrew the card from his wallet and slowly handed it over to the president. He watched with a sinking feeling of desolation as his right to publicly preach the word in SAB churches was taken away forever.

"I'm sorry about this, son, truly sorry."

***

Alone in his hotel room later that night, Christopher Hamilton stared out the window and watched traffic passing on both sides of the four lane highway. He'd driven to Dallas from Mississippi in response to the president's summons to a meeting. He hadn't had a clue that his employment would be terminated. He ministered, or at least he had ministered in Mississippi for the past seven years. Now he was without a congregation, without a job, and without prospects of getting one in this field. No ministerial credentials meant he couldn't work as an SAB pastor in any SAB church in the world. Christopher had never been good at accepting culpability. It was always someone else's fault if something didn't go right in his life or if his plan didn't unfold like he thought it should. He'd been poised to become the conference evangelist. Jethro Dent was retiring and had been rooting for him to fill the vacancy. Now all hope for that had been flushed away, and for what? Just because he gave women what they wanted? Just because they cried foul when he walked away?

If he'd gotten the job with Patmos in Mid-America seven years ago, he wouldn't have been here in this disgraceful position. But because of that slut named Brianna Robinson, that job had gone up in smoke, his dream job and the salary with it. Mid-America paid the highest pastoral wages. He'd ended up in some country district in Mississippi where the speech was more unintelligible than the language of immigrants and where his pay grade was class D instead of A like in Mid-America. Somebody was going to pay for his misfortune. He just lost everything—his position, his influence, and the respect of his colleagues. The news of his firing and the reason for it had flown fast around the conference in the three and one half hours since he'd left President Washington's office. Many were calls of condolence and even more were curiosity seekers wanting to get the 'juicy' details. A lot had been ministers who'd always been jealous of him professionally. He'd lost a lot today. Somebody would pay, he vowed again. And he knew who would.

CHAPTER IV

Seven Weeks Later

"Mr. H. says that we should respect and obey our parents, but if they want us to do something God doesn't like, we should pray and tell them the right thing."

"Sounds like a wise man," Brianna murmured, dividing her attention between Jonathon and the mail.

"Mr. H. says that we should not eat a lot of eggs," Jonathon spouted more of the gospel according to Mr. H., the new Bible teacher at his school.

"Ah, so that's why you wanted oatmeal this morning."

He smiled—that endearing and gap toothed smile that always made Brianna's heart feel quivery with affection.

"Is there anything else Mr. H. said before you eat the last of your oatmeal and go brush your teeth?"

He nodded and Brianna grinned. Why had she bothered to ask? The new Bible teacher, a substitute filling in until the regular teacher, Mrs. Wright, returned from maternity leave, had been there three weeks. In that short time he must have made quite an impression because Jonathon couldn't seem to stop talking about him and all his sage advice. Now his first homework was Bible. Brianna didn't mind. More about Jesus, like the hymn's title, is what people, and in particular kids, needed growing up with the many secular distractions in this world.

"He says that we can have cake and ice cream on Friday if the whole class can recite the sixty-six books in the Bible."

Mr. H. was allowing cake and ice cream into his class? Weren't those as bad as eggs, which he was against? Aloud she said, "Well you already know your Bible books; so it will be a breeze."

"Some people don't know them. *All* of us must know them for us to get the treat."

"Well, I'm sure you're going to be a good citizen and help those who don't know them to memorize, right?"

He nodded vigorously and got off his chair. "I'm helping Candy and Marie. They don't go to church; so they don't know the books."

"Good boy," Brianna encouraged him. "Now go brush your teeth so that we can leave for school."

"Okay, Mommy," he said and ran off to the bathroom."

Brianna took his oatmeal bowl and hers to the sink and washed them. She glanced at her watch: eight o'clock. Had Bart left for work already? He had to get there at nine. She hadn't heard him come downstairs. He usually stopped by to say he was leaving. She turned off the faucet when she heard a knock on the door. That would be Bart.

"Hey, Brianna," he called as he came towards her from the front of the apartment.

She turned, drying her hands in a dish towel. "Good morning. I thought you'd left."

"Daddy!" Jonathon flew out of the bathroom into Bart's open arms.

"Hey buddy. Ready to go to school?" He stooped, hugged him, and then sat back on his heels. "Got some toothpaste right here, bud," he told Jonathon, tapping the left corner of the child's mouth.

Jonathon wiped the back of his hand across the spot.

Bart laughed and Brianna made a face. He stood and took hold of Jonathon's hand. "Come on. Let's clean you up properly."

Brianna watched his retreating back from her position at the sink. His body wasn't body-builder muscled, but his toned frame was fit and strong. The shortest of all his brothers at five feet five inches, he always joked that God didn't have sufficient height left when he came along; so he got beauty instead. While a joke, Bart had a youthful and endearing face which Brianna never got tired of privately admiring. His toasty brown complexion—token from his Jamaican mother—were startling with his blue eyes—a gift from his Caucasian father. Bri coveted his thick eyelashes. His dimpled cheeks and that faint cleft in his chin topped off his great looks. When Tanya, a fellow trainer from her job, met him for the first time, she pulled Brianna aside and said she shouldn't bring him around with all the female, single trainers in the place unless she wanted to start a mob. Brianna had laughed because she knew women found Bart attractive. She did, which was pretty amazing after what happened to her with Jonathon's dad. Christopher Hamilton had been a fraud, masquerading as a Christian, and a pastoral student to boot. He'd denied outright that they had slept together when he found out she was pregnant. Brianna had cut her losses and committed to raising her son solo. That's when Bart had come along.

"We're clean and ready to go." The voice of the man she'd been thinking about interrupted her reverie as he returned to the kitchen with a clean-faced Jonathon. "See you later, Jon," he said, chucking the child under his chin.

"Later, Dad," Jonathon answered, retrieving his blazer from the back of the kitchen chair.

"See you, Brianna." He leaned in like he always did to kiss her cheek.

This time she shifted her head. This time his lips landed on hers. He pulled back fast like she were fire and he the burn victim. His eyes searched hers, and Brianna guessed the message she was broadcasting, *I want you*, killed the 'I'm sorry' on his lips. As the last syllable on the apology faded away, she saw his Adam's apple head for the hills and then slide to the valley.

"Jonathon," he said huskily, "Go upstairs and get my red pen off the night stand. If it's not there, check the coffee table."

"Okay, Daddy." The little boy ran off to do Bart's bidding.

Brianna ran her tongue over her lips, not because they were dry but more from the nervousness causing jitterbugs in her midsection. She hadn't meant to orchestrate a kiss…well not exactly true. Tired of pretending that this friendship with Bart was just a platonic one, she'd been thinking for some time now that she needed to take some initiative to move it to another level. Or at least, she needed to give him a clear signal that he had a green light to express an interest as more than a friend. With that thought increasing in strength every day, what she just did was a normal progression of thought manifesting itself into action.

Bart cleared his throat, and Brianna lifted her gaze from the knot in his silk tie to meet his eyes. His expression both questioning and hopeful, he said, "He'll soon figure out there's no pen and come back. Before that happens, I've got to ask you something Brianna."

She nodded since he seemed to want a reply in that pause.

"Do you want to move this relationship to a higher level?"

The knot in his tie became a fixation point again. Brianna felt suddenly shy and just a bit shaky at the thought that seven years plus after the first disaster, she was opening herself up to a new affair of the heart. This was an entirely different man, a caring, loving, considerate, and wonderful man. Knowing that and wanting to wait no longer for him to be hers, she had only one answer to his question. "Yes."

"Look at me Brianna."

When she looked up, he was smiling.

"I want you to see me coming in to finish the kiss you started."

She smiled then, a slow, inviting movement of her mouth, to let him know that they were united in that idea. She kept her eyes open until their breath mingled and closed them when his lips touched hers. The feel of him was heavenly and his taste intoxicating. His flavor, cool mint and cinnamon, fueled her hunger for more of his kisses. His firm mouth moved with stealth over her mouth. His lips whispered across hers like a gentle breeze across a plain. The sensation of those fleeting brushes gave Brianna a shivery feeling inside. Her limbs started feeling like melted ice cream oozing down the side of a cone.

She pressed her lips against his, asking for more intimacy. He gave it, intensifying the kiss into a deeper, longer, and stronger caress. His mouth steady and moving with focused intent now, Bart kissed her like a man on a mission to take everything she had to offer and then some. His lips became insistent, and his advance more determined. Bri felt her heartbeats quicken in response to his urgency. The pressure without matched the pressure within, and she shifted in his arms at the fast building tightness in her most private place—

her response to the heady stimulation of his lips seducing her. A long, feline purr escaped from Brianna.

Responding to the sound of her pleasure, Bart embraced her more intimately. His hand slid down her spine, the movement a sensual journey of tantalizing brushes, erotic touches, and intense caresses. Laminated against him like spandex to skin, Brianna experienced every dip and swell of his muscles and every angle and plane of his body. And when his touch traveled beyond the tip of her spine, his name escaped her lips, eddying out on a sigh, aching with desire for something beyond what they were sharing.

Trembling with a need to explore his body and touch him in the way he'd touched her, Brianna caressed his back in a southward glide, moved past his waist, and kept sliding downward. She smiled against his lips as his groan told her how much she was affecting him. Shifting her hands behind him once more in a now deliberate move, she elicited the response she'd been aiming for, that rumble of pleasure that her touch teased out of him. "Do that again." Brianna started to comply with his hoarse command and stopped mid-action at the sound of Jon's footsteps coming downstairs.

With reluctance they let each other go. "We'll talk tonight," Bart said his voice raspy.

Brianna nodded but wondered if they'd get much talking done with all the feelings the kiss had stirred up inside her. What she wanted to do much more than talking was to touch him, and kiss him, and hold him, and savor how good it was to be in his arms now that their affection for each other was out in the open. "Okay," she agreed softly.

"Bri if you keep looking at me like that, I'm going to send Jon back to look for more pens."

Brianna felt the heat rising in her face. His tie became her focus once more. She could only imagine that the yearning in her heart was plastered all over her face. "Sorry," she mumbled.

"Don't be," he soothed with a low laugh.

"Daddy, I didn't find it," Jonathon stopped beside them with the complaint.

"It's okay, Jon. I just remembered that it's in my bag." He smiled at the boy. "I've got to get going. I'll see you both later." The look he sent Brianna was full of want and mirrored exactly what she felt. "Later, Bri." The sound of his voice made her think of moonlight, hot bodies, shallow breaths, and the tropics.

"Later," Bri said, smiling at him coyly. And because she wanted to touch him, she reached up and pretended to straighten his tie and ended up smoothing her hand down his chest all under the guise of tie fixing.

"Bye," he said again. He reached out and brushed her cheek like he couldn't help touching her, before heading out of the apartment.

CHAPTER V

Brianna walked into Grace SAB Christian School to drop Jonathon off and to pay his monthly tuition. Curious about the popular new Bible teacher whom she only knew as Mr. H., she asked the school secretary, Paula, "Is Mr. H. here?"

Paula Hayward perked up at the sound of his name and her expression turned sly. "Heard about him, huh?"

Brianna looked at the young woman and wondered why she was wiggling her eyebrows in that way. "From my son, yes," she admitted.

"Oh," Paula said, her features changing fast from playful to professional. "I thought you'd heard..." She seemed to catch herself and aborted the sentence. Then as if she couldn't help it, she whispered in a rush with all the drama of the back of her hand to the side of her mouth, "It's just that he's very attractive and all the single ladies, teachers and parents alike, are gushing over him." Switching hats from gossip girl to poised professional, she said in a business-like way and with a smile that would put any hostess or receptionist to shame, "Yes, Mr. Hamilton is here, Ms. Robinson. Would you like to speak with him?"

"Yes, please." At least one mystery was cleared up. She'd

only heard of him as Mr. H. Now she knew his last name was Hamilton.

"One moment." Ms. Hayward held up a forefinger, lending action to her words, while she dialed an extension. "Yes, Mr. Hamilton, good morning. Ms. Robinson, Jonathon's mother is here. She wishes to speak with you." Ms. Hayward listened for a while then covered the mouthpiece. "Was it something specific that you wished to speak with him about, Ms. Robinson?"

"No," Brianna shrugged, "I just wanted to meet him. I haven't since he started here, and I like to see the faces of those teaching my child."

Ms. Hayward smiled in understanding and relayed the message to Mr. Hamilton. After some beats of silence, she said 'okay' and hung up. "Have a seat, Ms. Robinson. He'll be with you shortly."

Brianna sat in one of the four chairs in the small reception area of the school's main office. Grace SAB Christian School was a part of the Tri-State Conference of Churches SAB Educational system. Jonathon had started Pre-K here. He was now in third grade. He was ahead in the system. At age six plus—he'd be seven in November, a mere month away—he should have been in second grade but with the aptitude he'd shown in first, he'd been given second grade assignments simultaneously. As a result he completed two years in one.

She checked her messages while she waited. She didn't have to be at the gym until eleven o'clock on this Wednesday morning. She had a private client at ten o'clock so until then she was free. It was eight forty-five now. She scrolled through her text messages. Her mom, Julia, checking on her as usual; Tanya out sick again. Brianna thought of ignoring the HELP ME PLEASE request, suspecting Tanya wasn't at all sick but calling in because her boyfriend who worked with a cruise line was in town for a few days. Tanya very likely was hanging out with him. Brianna texted back to say she would only cover two of the girl's five classes for the day. She had to call somebody else. Tanya replied at once with a THANK YOU and a smiley face. The last text was from Bart, and her heart rolled like a wave and did a summersault when she read it. Her hand to her mouth to cover the sounds of tenderness threatening to become audible, she scanned the text again: *Hey Bri, just got to work and it's going to be an unproductive day. U know why? I can't stop thinking about you. Promise me you'll end my day the way you started it this morning.*

Brianna giggled at that part.

Who can concentrate on wills and trusts when an image of you is so much better?

Awww. Her heart went from mashed potato tender to melted butter soft. Bart was an estate planning lawyer working with a law firm in Lake Success, New York.

Can't wait 4 tonight. lots of luv. Bart.

Bart, her Bart. Her mind went dreamy. As she texted back *can't wait 2.* Brianna knew she was in love with Bartholomew Aaron Roach. She hit send, a soft smile still on her lips, at the same time someone said, "Ms. Robinson?"

Brianna looked up. Her smile died, and her heart jumped to her throat. Her mind started swimming from shock rather than the previous dreamy softness. In the nethermost place of her brain, his name registered; but she would have known him even if he hadn't said it. Christopher Hamilton! Jonathon's biological father! He was the *Bible* teacher?

"Ms. Robinson, let's step into the library. This way our talk won't disturb Ms. Hayward." Brianna watched him flash the school's secretary that lady killer smile, same one that had snagged her years ago, and watched the woman succumb to it, practically going cross eyed and smiling like a dimwit. Brianna got up abruptly and headed for the library across the lobby, not because he'd suggested it, but because she didn't want anybody to hear what she had to say to him.

The library was an oblong room with a square desk, four chairs and wall to wall shelves full of books. Brianna spun to face Christopher Hamilton as soon as the door clicked closed behind him. "What are you doing here?" she demanded, her tone hostile.

"I teach Bible."

"Aren't you in the wrong profession?"

"I left preaching."

"Left or were kicked out?" she derided.

Bri's heart faltered with uncertainty at the quick flash of pain she saw in his gaze before he hid it with lowered eyelids. His hands fisted and he took a breath, a noticeable one before answering.

"I know I deserve that and worse from you, Brianna. Though you won't believe it, I've changed."

She couldn't help the snort. Changed? Really? From skirt chasing, fornicating, and impregnating women and then denying paternity? The flash of softness she had felt for him disappeared with those memories of how he'd denied her pregnancy and refused to be a father to Jon. "I don't want you doing anything with my son, telling him anything except as it relates to your teaching him Bible. I don't want you revealing who you are because I'll call you a liar. You won't have a leg to stand on because you didn't claim him when you should and didn't want him when I gave you a second chance with the Intent to Adopt Notice. I—"

"What notice? What are you talking about? I didn't get it."

"It was delivered to you via FedEx. You signed off on it; so I know you got it." With his silence and him looking away, Brianna knew his protest had just been a bluff. And to think for a moment she'd felt sorry for him with that flash of pain—more like a false flash.

"What I should have said was I didn't read it in time."

"Oh, so something came to you via express mail, and you just left it lying around instead of opening it immediately? You expect me to believe that?" She raked him with a scornful look. "I may have been a gullible young girl once, but that innocent person is long gone Christopher."

"I'm sorry I destroyed that in you," he apologized humbly.

Brianna was not about to give him that kind of power over her—to make him think he had any type of influence over her perspectives. "Please don't take credit for that because what you did didn't harm me in any way. I didn't let it." Suddenly she wanted to make it very clear to him that she was over him; that what he'd done hadn't restricted her life in any way; and that she was whole, healthy, and very happy. "God is in the salvaging business. What you meant to be harmful, rejecting my pregnancy with Jonathon, God turned into something good. I met a wonderful man after the debacle with you. His name is Bart Roach and he *is* Jonathon's father. He was by my side through every pre-natal visit, through every pediatric visit, and knows what it means to be up all hours when Jon was sick. So Jonathon has a father even though you rejected him, and a very good one, much better I think than you could ever be."

The last was intentional, and so his flinch wasn't unexpected. She felt no sympathy this time.

"I'm glad for you and glad for Jonathon," Christopher said. "You have nothing to worry about. I won't be telling Jonathon who I really am."

"You had better not." If he expected her to be grateful, he'd better think again.

"I won't," he reiterated. "Earlier you doubted whether I was a teacher. I do have a master's degree in Education. I got that after I got my bachelor's in theology. I got out of ministry because like you my president didn't believe that I'd changed."

"Excuse me?" Brianna wasn't following him.

"There was a woman who claimed I'd slept with her, and the president believed her because of my past. I told him like I told you that I had changed, but he didn't believe me. Out of a job, I ended up here when this temporary position opened up. I had no idea that Jonathon attended this school. I didn't come here because of him, and I'm not here to make trouble or interfere in your life Brianna. I blew my chance. He's a smart boy, very respectful and very sweet. He loves you and his father a lot—talks about you all the time. In the few weeks I've known him, I'm not going to lie, I've had regrets and thought about many 'what ifs.' What if I'd made a different decision? What if I hadn't lied and denied that I'd gotten you pregnant? Maybe I could be proudly saying every time he repeats his memory verse, every time he helps a classmate, and every time he says, "yes, Mr. H." in that respectful way of his, that this is my son. But that's somebody else's honor now."

Brianna hadn't expected the shift in her heart or the feeling of pathos that suddenly stole over her. But there was a haunting aura surrounding his words that sounded like regret and an atmosphere of sadness that made her think that maybe, just maybe Christopher Hamilton wasn't the lowlife that he had been seven years ago. Feeling confused all of a sudden, she said, "I have to go." Side-stepping him, she made it to the door when the low sound of her name on his lips stopped her.

"Brianna." The sound was entreating.

"What?"

"Can I talk with you after work today?"

"Why?" She turned to him warily.

"I-I need a favor of you."

"And what makes you think you're entitled to favors from me?" she demanded, going militant with a hand on her hip.

"I'm not entitled to anything, Brianna. I'm just asking this as a favor, more like begging you. I need to ask you something."

"Ask me now."

"I can't."

"Forget it." She turned away. She wasn't going any place with this man ever again. The last place she'd gone with him she ended up pregnant and alone afterwards. Not that that would ever happen again. Only one man appealed, and the guy behind her wasn't him.

"Bri, please. If you want me to beg I will."

If she wanted? She turned around to blast that she wanted nothing from him. Her mouth stayed open, but no words came.

Christopher Hamilton was on his knees with his hands clasped in prayer in a gesture of entreaty. "Please, Brianna, I need your forgiveness."

"Wh-what are you doing?" She stuttered, shocked and embarrassed. "Get up before somebody comes in here and sees this."

As if on cue, there was a knock on the door and the lock jiggled. "Mr. Hamilton, this is Mrs. Garner. Are you there? Your first session has started and the children are waiting."

Oh, Lord. It's the principal, Brianna thought. How would she explain this? The man looked like he was proposing! "Get up Christopher!" She urged, taking him by the arm in an effort to get him back on his feet fast.

"Will you see me after work?"

Brianna looked into his coffee eyes so dark a contrast to his chocolate brown complexion. Jon had his coloring, but took the rest of his features from his grandmother. Was he trying to pull something? But the earnestness in his face and the sincerity in his eyes said otherwise. Brianna cast a frantic look behind. The doorknob was turning, which meant the principal was coming in. "Okay," she agreed because it was either that or explain to Mrs. Garner what was going on in the library.

He stood by the time the woman got in. He extended his hand to Brianna and said, "It was nice meeting with you Ms. Robinson. I have to run to class now, but we'll keep in touch via email. With a wave and smile at both women, he left. Brianna said good morning to the principal and left the building, wondering what she'd gotten herself into by agreeing to see Christopher Hamilton.

CHAPTER VI

"So let me see if I get this. Christopher Hamilton shows up after almost eight years of absence, and he expects to waltz in and reap benefits that he didn't work for or build?" Bart was holding unto his temper by a strand of hair. He was still trying to grasp what Brianna had just told him. Her words just now had robbed him of the pleasure of her company that he had been anticipating all day. The candlelight intimate dinner he'd put together sat uneaten on the table. He'd lost his appetite, and she hadn't come home with one.

Mr. H., the Bible teacher whom Jonathon had been raving about all month, was none other than his biological father, and the same deadbeat who quit on Bri after getting her pregnant. His son thought the sun rose and set in his teacher who just happened to be his father. That fact did not set well with Bart. He felt like his digestion had reversed. Where had the man been when Bri and Jonathon needed him? Where had he been when Bri didn't have transportation to run her back and forth to the doctor? Where had he been when she'd started bleeding and thought she was losing Jonathon? Where had he been during her six hours of labor when she'd been in so much pain she gripped Bart's finger and twisted it so hard that she sprained it? Nowhere and now he wanted to get to know Jon better— whatever that meant? After a lifetime of absence the man expected to come in and steal his son's affection? Not over his dead or living body.

"It wouldn't be like that," Brianna said in a low voice.

"Then how would it be?" Bart demanded, looking at her with increasing impatience. Was she seriously considering letting the man get to know Jonathon outside of school? As what? What role did he plan to play in the boy's life? It wouldn't be father, not as long as he had breath in his body. "What would Jon call him? What would be his role in this preposterous scenario?" He pressed when she was slow to speak.

"I don't know." She held her head in her hands as if it ached.

Bart's entire body was aching, especially his heart. He'd given Brianna seven whole years of his life, hadn't looked at another woman, hadn't been interested, with the hope and expectation that some day when she was ready to receive male attention again, she would look to him. He'd hoped that she would grow to love him even half as much as he loved her. Now he wondered if all along her affections had stood still and remained with this family destroyer named Christopher Hamilton. Was that why she was entertaining the notion of him getting to know Jon? Was that really why she'd agreed to meet him at Henry's, the popular Queens, West Indian Restaurant, after work today? Did she still love the man after all these years? Jesus, if that was the case he had flown off an airplane without a parachute.

"I haven't thought that far ahead," she whispered, adding to her previous comment.

It sounded like she hadn't thought at all. Knowing it wouldn't come out right if he said that, he tried a different approach. "Brianna, Christopher Hamilton is a suave, oily-tongued talker. You told me that yourself. That's how he fooled you. He's got a glib tongue. How do you know all this isn't just pretense on his part? How do you know that he doesn't have an underhanded agenda? Good grief! How do you know this isn't payback? Didn't you tell me yourself that he lost the California pastoral position fresh out of school because of what he did to you? You said John told my dad, and dad called the president who'd offered Christopher the position." John, Bart's brother, was Brianna's stepfather. "Maybe in Christopher's mind, this is an opportunity to win your trust and to hurt you, pay you back for that."

"I hear all that you're saying, Bart; and I've been worrying that payback is his intent. But if you had spoken with him and heard him beg for forgiveness, your confidence in possible pretense would have been shaken too."

Bart closed his eyes briefly and blew out frustration. "Brianna, the man could be acting."

"I don't think he is, Bart. He cried and not crocodile tears."

"And you're an expert on real versus crocodile tears now?" he asked sarcastically.

She lifted her shoulders in a weak shrug. "It's more intuition than anything else. I also remember how indifferent and aloof he was years ago when mom, John, and I confronted him before his parents with what he'd done. This time he acknowledged his wrong, took total responsibility for it, and asked my forgiveness for that and for all his years of silence."

"How does he explain the silence? What about the Intent to Adopt Notice that he didn't respond to? If he is so interested in Jonathon, why didn't he respond then and try to block me from adopting him?" Bart hadn't wanted to get into the adoption bit and come across as high handed or laying down the law, but come on, he was Jon's father and it felt like she was trying to take that from him now that Christopher Hamilton had appeared and shed a few tears. Bri seemed to have bought this guy's excuses wholesale and was ready to give up all the stability they'd built for Jon and this family or was this just an illusion of family? They were like husband and wife— yet they weren't. The only part of their family triangle that was true was the parenting part.

"He said he was doing a crusade at the time, which had just started. He said he forgot about it. He didn't find the notice until it was too late."

"And you *swallowed* that too." His inflection intimated that she'd gone past gullible to idiotic.

"I don't appreciate your tone, suggesting that I'm stupid!" Brianna snapped, anger lacing her words.

Bart didn't feel like tiptoeing around her tonight. He didn't feel like putting her feelings first. He had been doing that in this whole relationship, acquaintanceship, or whatever in God's name was between them. It wasn't happening tonight. "I didn't suggest a thing," he said flatly. "If you feel stupid, you did that all by yourself."

She flew from her seat, and Bart wondered if she was going to take a swing at him what with the way she balled her hands into fists and pressed them atop the table. He kind of hoped she would. His aggravation needed some sort of physical outlet, and if she took a swing at him he wasn't going to take it docilely. He wouldn't hit her back. He wasn't like that, but he wouldn't put shaking some sense into her past his capabilities tonight.

"I think you'd better leave," she declared through her teeth.

He wasn't going anywhere. "I pay seventy-five percent of the rent for this house. I think I'm entitled to sit anywhere in this building that I see fit."

"Well that's my chair and this is my dining room table so find something else to sit on!" She shouted.

"You're going to wake Jonathon up," he warned.

"I don't care. You started this."

"I didn't start anything. You brought this mess in here tonight. I was prepared to have dinner and some intimate conversation with you based on what happened between us this morning. Now I find that instead of just the two of us, Christopher Hamilton has made what I thought was a promising twosome into a threesome!" He'd told her not to raise her voice, but Bart found that anger was rising in him like a tidal wave and the only outlet was to shout right now.

"What are you talking about? Threesome? What threesome?"

Her genuine confusion fanned the fire in him. "Are you in love with this guy, Brianna?" he demanded, jealousy at that possibility goading him on. "That would be the only explanation for you even going out with him."

"No!" she exclaimed, gazing at him as if he'd lost his mind.

Bart didn't believe her. The more he thought about it, the more he believed that love for this man motivated her giving him any consideration to enter their lives.

"Why did you meet him at Henry's then?"

"I told you. I was between a rock and a hard place with the principal almost in the room and him on his knees before me. I didn't want to have to explain what was going on so I said 'yes' on the spur of the moment."

"And now you want me to accommodate him, bring him into my life, and take my son from me? I'm sorry, Brianna, I'm not doing that. You can accommodate him all you want—God knows you've already done that."

She was a little thing, but she packed TNT in a slap. Bart shook his head, his ears still ringing. He blinked and managed to focus on her. Silent tears ran down her cheeks, and she had her hand pressed to her ribs like she'd taken a bullet to the heart. He felt as low and as filthy as the vermin crawling beneath the city subway, knowing he'd struck her a low blow. As hurt as he was for her even thinking about letting Christopher Hamilton back into her life, she hadn't deserved that comment. She'd made a mistake by having a child out of wedlock. She'd been re-baptized. She hadn't revisited her error. He shouldn't have either. "Brianna, I'm sorry. I shouldn't have said that," he apologized.

"Leave, please," she begged her voice hoarse with pain and tears. She turned away from him not acknowledging his apology.

"Brianna," he started again.

"Go, just go."

He left.

CHAPTER VII

Brianna sat on the sofa in her living room and pulled her knees up to her chest. Wrapping her arms around her feet, she rested her cheek on her knees and stared out the window through the partially opened curtain. The house sat on a corner lot so the neighbor to her right was across the street. A car rolled to a halt by the stop sign next to her house before quickly crossing the intersection. The city needed to replace the bulb for the street lamp at the corner. What little light it gave barely cut through the darkness. From her position on the sofa, Brianna noticed these things in a detached way. She hadn't been able to feel a thing for about a half hour now, ever since Bart's remark. All this time when she thought that the sun rose and set in him, when she believed him to be a different kind of man, when she had the idea that he was unique, that was how he thought of her? He believed she was an accommodating kind of woman— the type who gave it up. That had hurt. All these years he'd helped restore her self-respect by making her believe that he had high regard for her despite the wrong choice she'd made by having a child outside of marriage. But tonight when he'd dredged up her mistake he'd made her feel cheap, the way she'd felt after that night with Christopher, and the way she'd felt when Christopher said he didn't want her anymore. The tears started again. Alone, in the darkness of her apartment, she didn't try to stop them. Lord, Jesus, she felt so broken, so hollow, and to think that she had planned to tell him she loved him tonight. To think that she had planned to make their six-year paper marriage a real one tonight. Her eyes burned as floodgates opened and the tears ran faster and harder down her face.

***

Bart came downstairs the next morning and found the door to Brianna's apartment still locked. They always left the doors to their apartments open, giving each other free access to one another's space. He'd come back downstairs after her dismissal last night to apologize again and to see if they could fix things. The door had been locked then too. He had a key but chose not to use it, thinking he should wait until she was ready to let him in. It seemed she might never do that. Bart knocked and waited. When nobody opened the door, he used his key and let himself in.

Cracking it, he put his head in and called, "Hello, it's Bart."

"Daddy!" A chair scraped across tiles, and Bart heard Jonathon's feet slapping the floor, headed for the door.

"Jon! Get back here!"

Brianna's sharp reprimand came too late. The boy was already at the door. Bart bent, scooped him up, and returned the exuberant hug his son gave to him. Placing his briefcase beside the potted plant next to the door, he stepped over Ironman and a Bat mobile on his way through the living room to the kitchen. He stopped in the arched entryway, balancing Jonathon on his left hip. Brianna stood at the sink, her back to them.

"Good morning, Bri." He greeted her as usual, although his tone was more sober than normal. He wasn't sure of his reception with the fight still an invisible wedge in the air between them.

She didn't answer him. Instead she reached for the tea cup next to her and sipped from it, before setting it down carefully and turning on the tap.

"Mommy, daddy's here," Jonathon intervened in the silence. Bart could see the confusion in his big brown eyes at her non-response to his greeting. Quietly he prayed that she would keep their differences between them and not drag their son into it. By her behavior Jonathon was sensing that there was a problem.

"I know that he is," she finally answered the boy. She turned around without looking at Bart. He knew it was her way of making it clear that she was ignoring him, as if he hadn't understood that from her lack of response. His lips tightened.

"Go and brush your teeth," she told the child.

"I brushed already."

"Okay, get your book bag. Let's go to school."

"But it's not time yet, mommy," Jonathon protested in bewilderment.

"We're leaving early today."

"But—"

"Just do it!" she snapped. Jonathon flinched, and Bart cut in.

"Jon, go to your room a minute," he told his son, giving the confused child a reassuring smile.

"Stay right there!" Brianna contradicted him.

"Bri, don't do that, please," Bart cautioned, laying an entreating hand on her arm while trying to keep calm—although he was angry with her for frightening and confusing their son. She was the mature one here. Why was she dragging Jon into their adult disagreement?

"Take your hand off me!" she snarled at him, turning her anger on him. Bart preferred it directed at him rather than at Jonathon. He deserved it, not the boy. He shot a look at the child. Tears slid down Jon's cheeks. He let Brianna go swiftly and was at his son's side in a stride. Pulling him into his arms, he said, "Hey, buddy. Don't cry. Everything's going to be all right."

"B-but why did mommy yell at me?" he quavered, looking from Bart's face to Brianna's.

Bart could not answer that and silently willed Brianna to respond and fix this, at least with their son. She did. She moved to stand beside them. Still ignoring Bart, she spoke to the child, "Mommy is stressed honey. I didn't mean to yell at you. I'm sorry."

"Do you still love me?" The question twisted Bart's heart, and when he looked at Brianna, he saw the shimmer in her eyes. She blinked.

"Yes, Jon, I love you very much," she spoke in a hoarse whisper, obviously trying not to cry.

All this was happening because they had both disregarded the Scripture and had let the sun go down on their wrath. He released Jon so that Bri could hug him and prayed while she did that that God would work things out between the adults.

"Go to your room, honey," she told the child. "I need to talk to daddy."

"Are you going to yell at him again?"

"I'll try not to," she promised.

At least she's honest, Bart thought. The smile she sent Jonathon was strained.

"Do you love daddy?"

He wished Jon hadn't asked Brianna that.

Instead of answering she said, "Go to your room, Jon."

Bart felt like his heart had dropped from his chest to the floor in less than a second. Did that evasion mean she didn't? God, he hoped not.

"Okay," Jon agreed and moved to obey. Half way to his room he turned back and asked, "Daddy, do you love mommy?"

"I love her," Bart declared without hesitation, meaning it one hundred percent while giving reassurance to his son. That put a full smile back on the child's face. With a happy skip and hop, he went into his bedroom and closed the door.

"You liar!" Brianna hissed as soon as the door clicked closed.

"Bri, can we not fight please?" Bart pleaded. He wanted to work the problem out, not escalate it. With fury flashing in her eyes, it didn't look like they were heading towards a solution.

"You should have thought about that *before* you called me a slut," she said scornfully, walking away.

Bart flinched. He hadn't used that word, but saying she was 'accommodating' was a short distance between the two. He followed her into the living room and apologized again, "Brianna, I don't know how many ways I can say 'I'm sorry', but I truly, truly regret that thoughtless statement last night. It was stupid and callous and I shouldn't have said it. Please, Bri, please forgive me." Bart stopped behind her, wanting to touch her but not knowing if she would go off on him if he did. The stiff way she held her body screamed 'back off' and 'don't touch me'. Literally she'd told him the latter in Jon's presence and with such violence that Bart had a feeling that she'd repeat the same if he put his hands on her again.

"What are you even doing in my apartment?" she

demanded, disregarding his apology. "The door was closed. Can't you take the obvious hint? It means keep out. Now get out! And stay out!"

"Bri, let's not part like this. I made a mistake last night. I wish I could take the words back—wish I'd never said them, but I didn't mean it." He took the risk and settled his hands on her shoulders. "Bri, you've got to believe me. I love you."

She wrenched herself stormily from his hold and whirled on him, an inferno blazing in her gaze. "You evil, despicable hypocrite," she growled. "Don't you dare tell me you love me because you don't. If you had you'd never have said that to me last night. What you said is just a mirror image of what you really believe about me." She stopped and tried to catch breaths shortened by agitation. "You spoke what you feel about me from your heart. If you didn't think me an accommodating woman you wouldn't have called me that."

"Bri, I—,"

"Shut up! Just shut up. I don't want to hear you and I don't want to see you. From now on, when my door is closed, don't come in. Even when it's open you're not welcome in here. I—,"

"Brianna, don't do this. You know you don't want this. You're angry and I can understand, but don't crush what we have when it's just blooming."

"Just blooming? From your perspective it was just blooming. I was just settling for what I thought I had to."

"What?" Bart's mind reeled and floated like he was recovering from a blow to the head. Settling? What did she mean? That she had accepted him because there were no other choices? Fear caused his heart to pound against his rib cage and his mind cried out to escape the annihilation Brianna's next words would unleash. And from the way this conversation was going, Bart suspected total destruction was only a Brianna word away. "W-what do you mean?" he asked unsteadily, trying to breathe around the trepidation tying up his throat.

Her face contorted with venom, she spat, emphasizing and pacing her words for maximum impact, "I never wanted you. You were right last night. I still love Christopher. He did me wrong but now he's back and begging for forgiveness. The love in me never died and I'm going to give him a chance." She raked a disparaging look over him from crown to toes. "I was grateful to you for all you did for me and Jon, but I never loved you. Your words last night gave me the excuse to get out of something I was going to get involved in because there was no other choice at the time—making you my husband in the full sense of the word. I want a divorce. By adoption law, you are Jon's father, but as of today, you are dead to me."

She marched to the front door and wrenched it open, "Get out!"

Bart was operating in two spheres: denial and truth. One side of his brain told him this was a dream. A section of his brain said that it wasn't really happening, that Bri hadn't just demanded a divorce, and that she hadn't in essence told him she never wanted to see him again. The other side heard every word, rapid, repetitive, and deadly like gunfire in a battle. Like bullets, her words hit him, every organ in his body taking their fire. But the worse casualty was his heart. It hurt—the pain of it was intense and unrelenting. It felt like his entire being was under attack and as if he were being shredded to bits in a long, excruciating torture.

"I'll go tell Jon, I'm leaving," he said stupidly, not knowing why he said that but turning to act on his words.

"No!" she commanded irately. "Get out, now!"

Feeling disoriented, he turned back to obey her. He was abreast of the door jamb when he snapped. This was what he got for seven long years of love and faithfulness and dedication to this woman. For seven years she'd been the pied piper playing a tune that he danced to because he loved her. And this, THIS, was how she treated him. H-E-C-K No! Spinning, he dragged the door from her hand, kicked it shut, and grabbed her by the throat. He slammed her against the door and pressed his body hard against hers, trapping the hands which she'd raised to ward him off.

In her eyes he read fear where fury had been before. A bone deep satisfaction that he'd put it there ran through his body. She'd hurt him. Without care she'd destroyed him. Let's see how she felt on the receiving end of destruction. He brought his face close to hers, and bit out through his teeth. "You said I think you're a slut, and you're right. I said you're 'accommodating' and I meant it. Only a cheap type of woman like you would take filth like Christopher Hamilton back. Because you're cheap, this is what you deserve. And I *dare* you to scream."

***

Brianna stood behind the front door of her apartment, shaking, hearing the reverberations of the slammed main door of the house, echoing in the wake of Bart's exit. Holding both sides of her now button-less blouse together, she tried to clothe herself with the dignity he'd just destroyed. When she'd imagined them together, it hadn't been like this. The touch she'd anticipated hadn't been insolent and insulting like what he'd just subjected her to. Intimacy with him had been soft touches and gentle caresses. This—this had been a mauling. After what he'd just put her through she felt even cheaper than the classification he'd given her. In Spanish they called it 'puta'.

CHAPTER VIII

"Mommy, are you okay?" Jonathon asked, worry lacing his voice.

Brianna had stopped counting the question after the fifth one.

"I'm fine." She gave him a fast glance and a quick smile as she waited for the light to change at the intersection. They were on their way to his school.

"Where's daddy?"

At least the question had changed. She should be thankful for that, but she didn't want to discuss Bart. "He went to work." Well she supposed so.

"No, he didn't."

He was shaking his head when she glanced his way.

"His car was in the driveway beside the house," he explained.

Brianna hadn't seen it, which wasn't surprising with her emotional state. "Maybe he carpooled to work today," she offered, hoping to kill the talk about Bart.

"Carpooled?" Jonathon sounded puzzled.

"Went in somebody else's car," she explained, hitting the gas as she turned unto Sunrise Highway. Switching lanes, she took advantage of the faster moving right lane and practically tailgated the person ahead to prevent a determined motorist from cutting her off from the left. Brianna ignored the guy as he laid on his horn. The long, loud blare testified of the height of his anger.

"May I use your phone, mommy?"

"Why?" she asked distractedly, seeking another space switch in the heavy Thursday morning Queens traffic.

"To call daddy. I want to know if he's okay."

"I'm sure he's fine, Jon. You'll see him later when he picks you up." That wasn't true. From today, she was making alternative arrangements for Jonathon's pick up from school. She no longer intended to depend on Bart.

"But I still want to call him," the child persisted.

"No, not now," she answered shortly. She had no plans to call him from her phone ever again, and she didn't want Jon to either.

"Didn't you and daddy make up?" Jonathon asked, his tone taking on a hushed and fearful timbre.

"No." It didn't make sense to be dishonest. Sooner or later, he would figure out that the problem hadn't been solved. She didn't intend to talk to Bart, and figured after what he'd done, he wouldn't speak to her either.

"You mean God didn't fix it after I asked Him to." Jonathon's voice turned shaky with tears.

He'd spoken to God about this? Brianna's heart staggered at that. She stopped at the red light, glad it had changed just then. She turned to Jonathon as he spoke again.

"But I begged Him to!" he cried, his large, brown eyes shimmering in distress and his face crumpling in disappointment.

What could she say? How could she tell a six year old that

God answers prayers in His own time yet He's never late? How could he wrap his mind around that bit of reasoning? Could she even ask him to accept that when she didn't believe it? This wasn't something God could fix, not after what Bart had said and definitely not after what he'd done. Yet she had to tell him something. "Jon," she started, "sometimes God doesn't answer our prayers right away. Sometimes we have to wait."

"Why?"

"He wants to see if we really believe in Him. Sometimes we have to pray to God more than once for an answer to come."

"So, if I believe really hard and pray even harder, God will make you love daddy again."

Brianna was at a loss. She hadn't stopped loving Bart, which was disturbing. She was madder than a bull at him, but deep in her heart she loved him. Still unsure of what to say, she spoke nevertheless. "I never said I didn't love your father."

"You never said you loved him."

Be-beep! Be-beep! Beeeeeep! The report of multiple horns of impatient motorists behind stalled her response. Brianna stepped on the gas without replying to Jonathon, made a right turn on 147th Road and followed it into the community of Rosedale where Grace Christian School was located.

She walked Jonathon into the lobby and stooped so he could kiss and hug her. "I'll pray for you and daddy. Don't worry. God will fix this. He can fix everything," he whispered in her ear as he hugged her.

Brianna walked back into the morning sunshine without feeling its warmth or seeing its brilliance, the latter because water was welling in her eyes like a river about to overflow its banks. God can fix anything, her son said. But could He fix this?

CHAPTER IX

Brianna had worked at First Class Body Fitness Center since becoming a personal trainer. She'd known, Tanya for five of the six years that she'd worked there, the woman having joined the staff a year after Brianna. They'd become friends rather than solely professional acquaintances in the last three years. So when Brianna walked into the locker room that morning after dropping Jon at school, Tanya took one look at her and said, "What's wrong with you?"

Brianna didn't look at her always ebullient co-worker. "Nothing," she muttered, opening her locker and storing her go-bag with her spare clothes.

"You walk in without your trademark smile and not only that, you look like the world ended, Jesus came, and you missed Him."

"Since when do you know about the Second Coming?" Brianna asked, raising an eyebrow at her friend.

Tanya grinned. "I may not want you preaching the gospel to me, like you've tried to do before, but that doesn't mean I'm ignorant of it."

Brianna gave her a sober look and tried to side step her.

"Hey, hey, wait a minute. No 'oh, please, Tanya.' No eye roll or 'I'll pray for you'? What's wrong with you?"

"I'm not in the mood for jokes this morning."

"I can see that, but what spoiled your usually good mood? You argued with Bart or something?"

If it had been only that, maybe she wouldn't have crumbled and succumbed to tears in front of Tanya. But it was so much more, and the magnitude of the problem between her and Bart settled its full weight on her. Suddenly Brianna couldn't bear it. Her tears started falling

"Hey, hey, take it easy," Tanya said, touching her arm in both comfort and concern. "Here, sit down." She pulled Bri down unto a bench in the locker room. "Don't take it so hard, girl. It can't be that bad that you can't work it out," she soothed, hugging Bri and patting her arm.

But it *was* bad, and Brianna was not sure there was anything left to work out. She had said some terrible things to Bart. In retrospect now the reason for saying all those words seemed so trivial. She'd wanted to hurt him, to make him feel equal amounts of the pain he'd inflicted on her the night before with his thoughtless words. Now they were both in anguish, and the lies she'd told him, the boulders in the form of words that she'd thrown at him could not be recalled just like how his words and his final act couldn't be revoked.

"Do you want to talk about it?" Tanya asked after a while when the tears dwindled to rivulets of water rather than torrential downpours.

Brianna pressed her fingertips against her tightly closed lids and shook her head, not because she didn't want to talk but because she wasn't sure how to begin. Could she even bring herself to tell Tanya how Bart had man-handled her? She wasn't sure she could tell anyone that? "We don't have time for me to tell it all," she said.

"We can finish over lunch at Subway. Just get as much as you can off your chest before our first class." Tanya looked at her watch. "We have ten minutes."

"Bart and I had a fight," She started. "And so many terrible things were said and done this morning that I think we're headed for divorce."

"You're married!" Tanya exclaimed incredulously. "When did you get married? I thought he was just the guy upstairs who helped you with your kid."

Brianna looked at her friend. This might take until dinner to finish. She opened her mouth and started an explanation that needed more time than hours in a day.

***

Their lunch break was nearly up. At one o'clock sharp, Bri had run across the street with Tanya to Subway for lunch. The restaurant had been crowded, but they'd snagged one of the few tables in the place as soon as the previous patrons vacated it. With the semi-seclusion of a corner table, Brianna felt more confident that their conversation wouldn't be overheard.

"You said you made a mistake that you're not sure you can fix," Tanya started when Brianna stopped speaking. "I think you made two."

Brianna frowned at her friend.

"It sounds to me that you've taken your man for granted for far too long."

"But I never did," Brianna protested.

"You keep saying Bart has always been an understanding, nice, even-tempered, and an everything-rolls-off-the back type of person. Just because he's that way doesn't mean he doesn't have feelings. It doesn't mean things don't bother him, and it certainly doesn't mean he won't get angry."

"You make it sound like I've been inconsiderate towards him."

Tanya ate the last of her chicken sub. She swallowed and wiped her mouth. "Don't take this wrong, Brianna; but you have been. Let me ask you this. Has Bart ever refused you anything?"

"What does that have to do with anything?" Bri frowned at her friend.

"Has he?" Tanya persisted.

Bri thought about that a while and then shook her head.

"Has he ever not been there for you?"

"No." Where was Tanya going with this?

"Did you ever think that he wouldn't be there or wouldn't be understanding in any situation?"

"No."

"And that's why you spoke with him about Christopher Hamilton and his interest in getting to know Jon, right?"

"Right. Tanya, what's the point? What does any of this have to do with our fight and how he mauled me this morning?" She told her that part too. Tanya hadn't acted shocked, which surprised Brianna.

"Bri, didn't you think that you'd be hurting him, be threatening him by bringing or thinking of bringing Christopher Hamilton into your life again?"

"I wasn't bringing him into my life. I wasn't even committed to bringing him into Jon's life. It was just something I thought about because he seemed to have changed. I asked myself if it would be Christian to withhold Jon from him because of his past neglect. Honestly, I said to myself, if God forgave him for his negligence, how can I not? God expects his creatures to exhibit the same forgiveness he has extended to them. That's the only reason I entertained his request to get to know Jon. Nothing more. As for me threatening, Bart, it wasn't my intent. I didn't know that he would feel insecure. Jon loves him and so do I. Christopher Hamilton can't take that away from him."

"But did he know that? Did you tell him all that?"

"There wasn't time to talk about love. Things unraveled so fast, and anger brought things to an explosive end so quickly that saying something like that was the farthest thing from my mind."

"Did you tell him what you were thinking—your motivation for entertaining Christopher's request?"

"Like I said the argument escalated fast, and we were so angry that it never came up."

"It sounds like you owe him an apology."

"Me? Apologize?" Brianna glared at her friend, thinking that she'd wasted her time telling Tanya all her business, for the girl to give this foolish advice. "*He* needs to apologize!" She lowered her voice and leaned across the table. "He tore my clothes, he disrespected my body, and shamed me," she hissed.

Tanya studied her dispassionately for some seconds. "And you did nothing to bring about that disaster."

"Why would I invite that kind of thing on myself?" Brianna asked in annoyance.

Tanya sighed and sat up in her seat. She pushed her sandwich wrapper aside and placed her elbows on the table. "Brianna, I was married for three years. I learned a lot of what I'm about to say after I divorced. If I'd learned it before, I'd still be married. Now listen. You need to affirm your man and make him know the sun rises and sets in him. He needs to know that you love him through word and deed. It sounds like you haven't done that. I know your situation was a little peculiar with that paper marriage arrangement, although girl I don't know how you kept your hands off him all this time." She grinned and Brianna smiled a little. Sometimes it had been hard. "So you didn't tell him since it wasn't a real marriage, but you should have started out last night by telling the guy that you love him before you brought up Christopher Hamilton. I guarantee you, if you had, we wouldn't be sitting here and having this conversation. The next thing is that you NEVER, EVER goad a man, which was the second mistake you made."

"I didn't—." She stopped when Tanya held up her hands.

"Hear me out. You goaded him when you lied and said that you never wanted him, but always loved Christopher and wanted to go back to him. Bri, Bart is a human being with feelings. This morning the man admitted before your son that he loves you. For all these years like you told me he's been by your side. Do you think any man would do that just to be kind? He has feelings for you, Bri. He cares about you and loves you. That's why he did it. Now when you went with your stupid self—sorry but that suits you right now—and told the man how you love Christopher, shouted at him and told him to get out of your place, and then you turned around and denied him access to his son, he would not be human if he didn't snap. And don't even try to tell me about Christianity controlling his reaction. He's a human being, and it was just too much for him to take. Just like you hurt him, he hurt you. Tit for tat and all that."

Brianna didn't say a word after that. When Tanya broke it down like that, she could see how Bart had lost it. She swallowed, still trying to hold onto some of her indignation but the hollowness of the protest reflected the weakness of her ire, "But what about him suggesting that I sleep around."

"I thought you said he apologized."

"He shouldn't have said it in the first place."

"True. But weren't you considering forgiving Christopher Hamilton his mistake? What about Bart? Isn't he allowed forgiveness for a mistake?"

Brianna stared at Tanya stunned at her reasoning. Who was the Christian here again? The children of the world are wiser in their generation than children of light. Isn't that what the Bible said somewhere in Luke? Dear Father, she'd messed up big time. "Oh, God, Tanya. What am I going to do? How am I going to fix this?" she asked her friend desperately.

"Well you'd better call him first."

"Suppose he doesn't answer."

"Find out where he is and go there after work." She pushed her chair back and stood. "Now lunch time is over, and we've got to get back. Let's go."

CHAPTER X

On Thursdays, Jonathon had Bible just before lunch. At the end of class he went to his Bible teacher.

"Hi, Mr. H."

"Hello, Jonathon." Mr. H. smiled at him.

"May I ask you something?"

"Sure. Anything."

"Will you help me pray for my parents?"

Christopher Hamilton looked at the third grader sharply. Pray for his parents? Why? Were they having problems? Wouldn't that make his mission easier? He needed to find out if there was really a problem. Choosing his words carefully, he said, "Of course, Jonathon. Is there anything specific that you want to pray for?"

The boy nibbled on his lower lip before confessing in a lowered voice. "They fought this morning."

How wonderful. Aloud he said, "Sometimes parents do that."

Jon shook his head. "Mine never do."

Never? It must have been major then, if the boy had come to pray about it. "Okay Jonathon. Let me ask you a few questions so we can know what to say to God. Is that all right?" He smiled at the boy gently.

"Okay," Jonathon agreed.

"Are your parents talking to each other?"

He shook his head. "At least mommy isn't talking to daddy, but I don't know why."

Great, Christopher thought gleefully.

"Maybe your daddy did something and your mom needs to forgive him." Christopher made his tone mild and his remark more statement than question to cover his fishing expedition.

"I don't know what he did, but mommy didn't say she loved him when he told her he loved her."

Suddenly things clicked in Christopher's head. He would bet money Brianna had brought up the issue of him seeing Jon outside of school and getting to know him. Very likely, she and her husband had fought about that. A divided house could not stand. Inwardly, he gleefully rubbed his hands. Brianna was already emotionally injured. He would hit her when she was already weakened. The impact would be greater. He wasn't planning to let Jonathon know that he was his father, but he wasn't above putting a seed of doubt in his brain that Brianna's husband wasn't his real dad. First he had to find out if the boy knew he was adopted. Now was not the time, but soon.

"Can you help me to pray now, Mr. H.?"

"Certainly, Jonathon, certainly. Let's kneel," he invited.

***

That afternoon

Gail McPherson, partner at the Family Law Firm of Morgan and McPherson, considered the man who'd come in for their 'Exploratory Interview'. He wanted to know his options, he'd said over the phone, where exercising his paternity right was concerned. Now based on what he'd shared, he didn't have any rights to exercise.

"Mr. Hamilton, adoption in most states and in particular in

this New York state is irrevocable," she explained. "Unless there has been some fraud surrounding the adoption, then you cannot exercise your paternal rights over your son."

"I believe that fraud was involved. I didn't know that he was being adopted."

"I thought you said that you received a Notice of Intent to put your child up for adoption." Gail raised her eyebrows at him.

"I did but by the time I read it, it was too late."

Ignorance is no excuse, Gail thought privately. "Mr. Hamilton, did you ever visit your child or provide any type of support prior to him being adopted?"

"I didn't know about him, so I couldn't do that."

"How did you find out about him?"

"I teach at his school and met his mother yesterday. That's how I knew he was mine."

"So your child's mother admitted to you that the boy is yours."

"Yes."

Something didn't feel right to Gail. Why would the mother admit that the child was his seven plus years later? According to him they'd had relations a little over seven years prior. If the adoption had been fraudulent, wouldn't she have denied his parentage, knowing he could investigate like he was attempting to do now? Gail decided to dig a little deeper to discover this man's real motivation for wanting to exercise his paternity. "Now tell me who exactly has adopted your child. It seems he's still in the care of his mother; so who is the adoptive parent?"

"Her husband."

The disdain in his tone was very slight, but Gail picked it up. Was this sudden interest in his child motivated by bitterness? Or was it an attempt to get back at the child's mother for marrying another man? She wasn't getting a good vibe off this man. She had practiced law, family law, long enough to know better than to take anything at face value. Oftentimes the information submitted in these matters was incomplete and parents usually had ulterior motives in this area of law, especially as it related to adoption.

"You said you were unaware of your son's existence, Mr. Hamilton, but did you ever try to contact his mother in the last seven years just to verify if you had an offspring."

"No, why would I? We had broken up." He regarded her like she wasn't sensible. Gail's dislike for the man increased.

"If you had, you might have been aware of your son." She had to work hard to keep her tone professional rather than chiding. "And had you been aware, you could have supported your child in some way or attempted to do so."

"Attempted? Do you doubt that I would have?" His tone was silky and the question dangerous. Gail wasn't intimidated. That's why she thrived in her profession. She didn't cower easily.

"I don't know you Mr. Hamilton, so I wouldn't presume to know what you would have done. But I will tell you that had you tried to verify the existence of your child and attempted to establish a relationship with him, New York State would have looked at you favorably and considered you to have paternity rights."

Gail felt like she had wasted enough time with this person. He had no case and this was a free session. It was time to attend to paying client cases. She decided to give him the final facts and shut him down.

"Mr. Hamilton, in the state of New York, claiming ignorance of your child is not an acceptable reason for seeking to overturn an adoption. You cannot use a lack of awareness of your son's existence as a reason for not establishing paternity rights."

"But if I didn't know about him, how could I have established those rights?"

Gail noticed his voice had an edge to it, and his heavy frown spoke of his displeasure with her statement. "I don't write the law, Mr. Hamilton. I just practice in it." She flipped her iPad closed. This interview was pretty much over. He had no case and no leg to stand on. "In fact, under New York law, you weren't even entitled to receiving an Intent to Adopt notice. That probably was a courtesy that your son's mother extended to you." Gail pushed her chair back and stood. "I'm sorry Mr. Hamilton, but this firm cannot help you. Have a good evening." She didn't offer an exit handshake. She didn't shake the hands of people she didn't trust.

He rose without a word, but the look he leveled at her before he turned and left was full of contempt.

CHAPTER XI

It was after nine before Bart left the office. He'd worked late, not because he had to but because he didn't want to go home. He was so ashamed of what he'd done he couldn't face Brianna. She would not forgive him this. Maybe if she loved him, she would consider it, but in essence she had told him that she didn't. She already started severing their family relationship. Today was early dismissal at Jon's school. The school secretary said he'd gone home with a parent who lived close by. "Ms. Robinson," she said, "made that arrangement this morning." Ms. Hayward, the secretary, thought he knew. To hide the fact that he really didn't know about it, he told the secretary that he forgot. As he walked out of the school's office he thought, *She's cutting me out of Jon's life already.*

Several times today he'd wanted to call Brianna; but he couldn't, not only from fear of her rejecting him again but because he'd lost his phone to the city sewer this morning. After he left her apartment, he'd been so enraged, he just walked block after city block to work out his fury. When his anger subsided, it was way after nine in the morning. He'd taken his phone out to call the office and the device had slipped from his hand and fallen into the sewer. He hadn't wanted to call her from the office what with the nature of the problem between them so delicate and personal. And he wouldn't get a replacement phone until next week.

Bart made a decision as he walked into the now deserted parking lot of Shineman and Bonner Estate Planning PC. The distance to his parents' place going east into Long Island was the same distance as from the office to his home in Springfield Gardens, Queens. Exhausted, Bart slid into the leather seat of the Jeep Grand Cherokee and fired up the engine. A quarter mile away from his office he saw the signs for the east and west bound Northern Parkway. West led home and to a family that was no longer his. East led to his parents. He took the east bound ramp.

***

Half way to his destination, Bart stopped at his brother, Peter's house. As he knocked on the front door, he admitted that he'd done it because he needed to talk to somebody. He couldn't bring himself to bare his domestic affairs to his mom and dad. And Peter might be able to help him understand Brianna suddenly wanting to give Christopher Hamilton access to Jon. Peter had a son whom he didn't help to raise, not from choice but because the woman hadn't told him about the pregnancy. His son, Ashleigh, had introduced himself to Peter a little over a year ago. He knew Peter regretted not having seen the boy grow up. So maybe he could help Bart get some perspective on this whole Christopher Hamilton mess.

"It's Bart," he answered his brother's query for his identity.

"Hey, Bart, what's up?" His older brother greeted him, embracing him as he stepped into the foyer.

"I was passing by and thought I'd drop in and say hello."

"Hi, Bart." Pamela, Peter's wife came upstairs from the den.

"Hey, Pam." He hugged her too. "Hope it's not too late for me to drop by."

Pam fanned the thought aside with a flick of her wrist and an 'oh please' expression. "Can I get you something to drink or eat or both?" his sister-in-law offered.

"No, thanks, Pam. I'm not hungry."

"Okay, come sit." She smiled in invitation, walked into the living room, and sat on the sofa. "Peter and I usually catch Rachel Maddow on MSNBC around this time. All the kids are in bed, so this is our down time." They had four kids at home, including the latest addition to the family, Isaiah, a one year old. Pamela had been raising her two nieces and two nephews when she and Peter married. Her older nephew, David, was in college.

When Peter made to follow his wife, Bart detained him with a hand on his arm. "Hey, P, can I talk to you?" he asked, lowering his voice so Pamela wouldn't hear.

His brother gave him a curious look. "Sure," he said and headed downstairs to the den.

***

Bart sat next to his brother on the ash colored leather sectional sofa in Peter's den. How should he start? He wondered. Where should he begin?

"What's on your mind, Bart?" Peter prompted.

Bart rested his elbows on his knees, wrapped his right hand over his left fist, and perched is chin on his fisted hands. "Brianna and I are getting a divorce."

"I'm sorry. Say that again."

Bart caught Peter's bemused expression. He realized he

had just hit him with a shocker. None of the family members knew about his marriage to Brianna. They'd kept it to themselves since it was more business arrangement than the real thing. Bitterness and recrimination hit him at the thought that it had been on the point of being much more than that.

Peter straightened up from his relaxed position. "You and Brianna are married? How long?"

"Six years."

Peter whistled. "And you didn't tell anybody all this time." He paused and raised an eyebrow at his brother. "Or am I the last to know?"

"No, we didn't tell anyone."

"Why not?"

He explained that his marriage to Brianna wasn't one in the real sense. He talked with Peter about the adoption and deciding to marry to give Jon his name and to make the adoption process easier. Well, that's the story he told Peter and the one he'd given to Brianna; but Bart had married Bri because he loved her. And then he told his brother about Christopher Hamilton and the fights with Brianna. He stopped short of his last act before leaving the house earlier.

"This sounds like a colossal mess," Peter said.

"It's worse. There's more," Bart confessed and told him the rest.

Peter kept quiet a good while after Bart finished talking. Bart tried not to imagine the disgust for him that his brother must be feeling.

"It is worse," Peter finally said heavily. "It sounds like you lost your mind for a while."

"Every time it replays in my head, I can't believe I did that. I've tried to shut it down, but it keeps coming back—like a haunting. I can't understand how I lost control like that."

"Anger. It makes you do unnatural things. That's why we need to walk away from a situation that stirs it up."

"I did. At least I started to walk away; and then it was like something burst, more like exploded in my head and all I could feel was a boiling rage. I wanted to hurt her as much as she'd hurt me."

"And how do you feel now?"

Bart gave a disgusted snort. How did Peter think he felt? "Like crap, man. Total and complete garbage. God, Peter, I hate myself right now. I can only imagine she hates me ten times more. I don't think she'll ever forgive this."

"You need to ask God to forgive you first."

Bart emitted a mirthless laugh. "For a deliberate act of harm?"

"Are you sorry for what you did?"

"I'm so sorry I wish I could turn time back and erase the whole thing."

"That's what God's forgiveness is about—your repentance or expression of sorrow for a wrong. He knows you're sorry. Just talk to Him about it, and His forgiveness is yours. You know the drill. Once you've restored your vertical relationship with Him, then you can work on the horizontal with Brianna and ask her to forgive you."

"She wants a divorce, Peter. There's no horizontal relationship to work on."

"Anger makes us do and say stupid things. You're a prime example—both you and Brianna. I think she was just trying to hurt you for making her feel like crap last night."

Bart gave Peter a skeptical look. "You think so?"

"I think so."

"But why would she go so far as demanding a divorce if she weren't serious? Why would she even tell me that she loved this guy, Christopher, if she didn't? That's going a little far. Don't you think?"

Peter looked at his brother in amusement. "Bart, I don't understand why women do what they do or why they say the things they say. All of tha—"

"And why is she even thinking about bringing that guy back into her—our lives?" Bart interrupted. "Do you think I should have been more understanding instead of 'losing' it when she said that?" He shifted on the sofa so he could look at Peter more directly. "You had a son you didn't know about until late in life, and you felt the loss of not seeing him grow up. Hamilton's situation is similar to yours except he knew about Jon and chose not to get involved. Do you think Bri and I should accommodate his request to know Jon now? Or do you think he blew his chance?"

Peter raised his hands and shook his head in the universal 'I have no idea' sign. "Bart, you asked me so many questions that I don't know which to address first, and I'm not even sure if I can answer them all."

"Answer the one about whether I should agree with Bri's idea to let him see Jon."

Peter considered that. "That's a hard one. Like you said, I know what it is to miss out on my child's life, and it isn't a good feeling. Granted, I didn't know about Ashleigh. The thing is Hamilton knew about Jon and wanted no part of him. Probably he's truly changed now and wants to really know the boy. Then again, he might be trying to hurt your wife by getting close. It's your responsibility to shield her from harm. So I don't think you're wrong in wanting to keep him at a distance. The other thing is that the Bible calls a man who doesn't provide for his offspring and household an 'infidel'. He hasn't provided for Jon, although he knew about him. You did that. Through adoption you are Jon's dad. My final thought is sometimes there are no second chances in life. I think this situation is one of them."

Bart heaved a sigh of relief at his brother putting things into perspective so tidily. He really liked the gospel according to Peter.

"Now that your mind is resting easier on the Hamilton angle, may I go back to what I was saying earlier about your problem with Bri?" Peter asked.

"Sure. Finish your thought."

"I think that's more important than Hamilton right now."

Bart nodded in agreement.

"The fight and the harmful words that were said are in the past. They already happened, and you can't change the past. You can shape the future, and it looks to me like you want a future with Brianna. Otherwise you wouldn't be so broken up over this whole thing, right?"

"Right."

"Well you need to let Brianna know that in spite of all that happened you still care."

"Shouldn't I apologize first?"

"An apology is part of showing care."

"Peter I don't know if I have the guts to face her, to look her in the eye, after what I did." Bart shifted on the sofa, the thought of talking to Bri face to face making him uneasy. He was too ashamed of what he'd done.

"I'm not suggesting that you see her face to face. In fact I'd advise you not to do it right now in case she hasn't calmed down enough yet. Find some kind of bridge contact."

"Bridge contact?"

"You know, present yourself; reach out to her but not in person."

Peter rolled his eyes at his brother's blank stare. "Okay dunce bucket. Buy a nice card with some words of apology or better yet get a beautiful blank card and write your own apology. Do *not* send it through the mail. Send it UPS or FedEx overnight. You need to convey urgency and desperation for forgiveness."

For the first time that day, Bart smiled a genuine smile. He was glad he'd stopped by Peter's. "Thanks Peter. Where'd you get that idea? Used it before?"

"No." Peter shook his head, and then added with a grin, "But wisdom comes with age. So I know things that you, at only thirty two, can't even dream of."

Bart rolled his eyes at his brother's gentle teasing.

"But seriously, I don't know where it's coming from. It's likely the Holy Spirit sent it for your benefit. Write it down before you forget it. Oh, I forgot. Your phone is in the city sewer." Peter grinned.

"I won't forget. My future's riding on it."

"Moving on," Peter continued. "That's day one. On day two, send a single rose and on day three, pull out the stopper and buy the most expensive bouquet in the flower shop. If the FedEx package didn't come back by day three, I think it's safe to see her in person."

"Thanks, P, I'd never have thought of these things on my own because all I kept hearing is 'I want a divorce'."

"Don't thank me until it works," Peter cautioned but with a smile, rising from the sofa as Bart stood.

"I'm going to stay by mom and dad for a few days."

"That's wise at least until the dust settles."

"Thanks again, Peter." Bart hugged his brother, and Peter squeezed him close.

When they separated, Peter rested a hand on his brother's

shoulder. "Let's pray before you go."

Bart bowed his head and closed his eyes, grateful for the thought.

"Dear Lord, we thank you for another chance to talk to you. We ask for forgiveness of sin; so the way to heaven will be clear for this prayer to go through. Lord at creation you made two things that the devil keeps attacking: the Sabbath and marriage. I pray for Bart and Brianna and their marriage. There's division, confusion and anger in this union right now. Lord, I'm praying for healing for this marriage. I'm asking you to manifest yourself in Bart's heart and in Brianna's too because your presence brings order and peace. Lord, as your Spirit brings them peace, draw their hearts back together; heal the hurt, the friction, and the strife that brought division between them. And Lord, after your restoration and healing, may they praise you for the wonderful thing you have done. I ask these blessings in the name of Jesus. Amen."

"Amen." Bart hugged his brother tightly, emotion working his throat muscles. "Thanks, man. Thanks."

"Anytime, bro." Peter hugged him back fiercely. From the strength of his embrace and the coarseness of his voice, Bart figured his brother was feeling pretty emotional too.

CHAPTER XII

When Bart wasn't home by ten, Brianna noticed. In truth she noticed since seven o'clock, but figured he'd worked late. By ten o'clock, she was concerned. He hadn't answered her several calls and her final phone call got a recording that said his phone was disconnected. Worry made her heart weak. She'd told him she wanted a divorce, although she hadn't meant it. Had he taken her seriously and was cutting off communication between them? It would seem so. Why else would he disconnect his phone? Plus he'd disconnected without telling her. Was that an overt message that he didn't want to hear from her ever again? She kept hope alive that it wasn't the case until ten thirty. After that she gave up that tenuous belief. She had allayed Jon's concerns with the assurance that Bart worked late which was why he wasn't home. He'd fallen asleep with the comfort that he'd see his father by morning. But with Bart absent and with no communication from him, Brianna didn't know what she would tell Jonathon in the morning.

At eleven fifteen her will overcame her resistance to call family about his whereabouts. By eleven thirty, none of his brothers had seen him nor heard from him. The only person she hadn't reached was Peter. Brianna didn't leave a message on his machine. She didn't call his parents because it was too late. She finally crawled into bed after midnight. Bart still hadn't come home. She had even checked his apartment in case he'd gotten past her open apartment door, which she had been steadfastly watching since Jon went to sleep. Pulling her comforter over her head to stifle her sobs, Bri flooded her pillow with frustrated and unhappy tears.

***

Brianna had just finished a training session the next day when her cell rang. It was Jon's school. Wiping sweat from her temple, she answered the call and headed for the locker room.

"Hello."

"Ms. Robinson, this is Mr. Hamilton."

Christopher! Why was he calling her? Matching his formality she replied, "Hello, Mr. Hamilton. How may I help you?" She hadn't called him about his request, and she didn't plan to. After the disaster that mention of his name had brought to her and Bart's relationship, Bri didn't think it was worth letting Christopher back into her life or Jon's. Even if he had changed, it wasn't worth it. He couldn't erase or explain away his years of silence. And her future, the one that included Bart—the man whom she loved—wasn't worth sacrificing for Christopher Hamilton. This was the consequence he had to bear for rejecting Jon from the womb. His choice then was like sin. It could be forgiven, but the consequences still remained.

"Ah," he said and hesitated before lowering his voice, "Can you bring a change of clothes to school for Jonathon, please?"

"What happened to Jonathon?" Brianna asked, her breath quickening with concern.

"He had an accident."

"What happened?"

"Calm down, Ms. Robinson. He's not hurt," he said in a soothing tone. "He's just wet. Something spilled on him and he needs to change."

"What got on him and who did it?" Brianna demanded, thinking that the school bully, Garth Morrison, had sprayed water on Jonathon again. Jon was skinny and not particularly tall for his age. Since the year started Garth had picked on Jon two times and all because Jon had gotten his attention when he stepped in and stopped the boy from bothering his friend, Melissa.

"Nobody did anything, Ms. Robinson. How soon can you get here with the change of clothes? I'll explain when you arrive. He's very wet and uncomfortable."

"I'll be there in a half hour," she promised, rushing out of the locker room and heading for the admin office to tell the manager that she had to run out on an errand. Her next client was due in fifteen minutes. She had to get someone to fill in until she returned. Tanya wasn't available. She tried Gabriela. The red-haired Venezuelan girl was new and still building her client base so she had more time in between sessions. She agreed to help Brianna. Brianna was grateful for the spirit of cooperation among the trainers at her gym. Many of the men and women who worked here had families with children. From time to time people had emergencies with their kids. They understood and helped to cover for one another.

***

Flying down Sunrise Highway, Brianna blew through more amber lights than she could count and a few red ones too if she were to tell the truth. She prayed to God no traffic cameras had picked her up because the fines would be more than she could afford, and she'd probably lose her license. Christopher had said that she shouldn't be alarmed, but only one thing other than somebody deliberately throwing water on him could make Jonathon wet and uncomfortable. Brianna tried not to believe it, but the thought wasn't going anywhere. Jonathon had overcome his bed-wetting problem since four years old. He couldn't have peed on himself, could he? Not at this age, right? Besides, that only used to happen at night when he was asleep. It was broad daylight, he was in school, and wide awake. So that could not have happened.

She tore into a parking space at the front of the school, not caring that her VW bug slewed across two spaces. She didn't run inside, although she wanted to. If Jonathon had indeed urinated on himself, she didn't want to break into crisis mode and rush in. That would call unnecessary attention, elevate curiosity levels, and probably have people poking their nose into his business. To convey calm, she shortened her ground-devouring strides to conservative steps, when she walked into the office and asked for Mr. Hamilton.

Christopher came quickly. "Hi, Ms. Robinson," he greeted her formally. "Jonathon is in the teacher's lounge," he revealed, lowering his voice. "Please come with me."

As they walked down the deserted hallway, he explained, "He fell asleep during Bible class. I had to wake him up twice. The third time I just let him sleep. Isn't he feeling well?"

Pain squeezed her heart at the question. No he wasn't, but because of sadness, not sickness. Bart not coming home last night caused Jon's despondence. She could imagine that he hadn't slept well either, which was why he'd fallen asleep in school. "He's not sick," she allowed. Brianna didn't want Christopher knowing about the fight between her and Bart. She hoped to God Jonathon hadn't mentioned it.

"Is everything all right at home?"

Brianna stopped and swung to face him, her heart

pounding. Did *he know? Had Jon said something?* "Why do you ask?" She inquired evenly, just managing to keep her rising panic under control. She did not want Christopher knowing her business.

"Brianna, since yesterday, Jonathon hasn't been himself."

"What do you mean?" She held her breath.

"He's been abnormally quiet, even withdrawn—he hasn't been participating in class. The Language Arts teacher mentioned the same thing to me this morning, wanting to know if I'd noticed. Now he's fallen asleep during instruction. For a child to change in behavior overnight there has to be a reason." He stopped, hesitated a moment, and then added, "I didn't want to mention this, but he asked me to pray for his parents yesterday."

Brianna closed her eyes. Oh, God, he knew. How much? It didn't matter. The excruciating and embarrassing part was that he knew there was strife and friction between her and Bart. Christopher Hamilton was the last person she wanted to know about her domestic problem especially after she boasted to him on Wednesday morning about what a great guy and dad Bart was. Now for sure, he would gloat that the perfect picture she'd created was far from that.

She opened her eyes, expecting to see a smile of satisfaction on his face. There was none. She searched his gaze with intensity but could find nothing but concern in it. Did he truly care about Jon's welfare? Was he really not rejoicing in her unhappiness? Was the old Christopher really gone—the callous, indifferent one who wanted nothing to do with her after taking her innocence and ditching her with a pregnancy?

"Is everything all right Brianna?"

The gentle question, full of sincere interest, touched the chords of unhappiness in her soul. She had to turn aside so he wouldn't see her tears. A white handkerchief fluttered next to her cheek. Brianna took it and mopped her eyes. Life was interesting. Her enemy had become her empathizer. That was a pretty incredible picture. Just how incredible she would later find out.

***

At the teacher's lounge door, Christopher offered, "I'll give you privacy with him, but if there's anything you need or anything I can do, please let me know."

With those few words, Brianna looked into Christopher Hamilton's face and found once again what had first drawn her to him—warmth, friendliness, and convincing interest in another person, not to mention his chocolate brown and handsome good looks.

"Thanks, Christopher. I appreciate it." She smiled at him, opened the door, and stepped into the teacher's lounge.

***

When the door clicked closed behind Brianna, a slow smile of predatory satisfaction stole across Christopher Hamilton's lips. Brianna Robinson's perfect and happy world was crumbling. With what he'd told the First Elder of her church last night, it would be totally destroyed come tomorrow. He walked back to his classroom whistling.

He found a note from Ms. Hayward on his desk. *Tonight?* One single word and a punctuation mark widened his smile. He wrote 'yes' with a plan to drop it on her desk on his exit from work later. He didn't mind accommodating her. After all she had been more helpful than even she knew. Unwittingly, she'd given him access to the students' records. Tonight would give him a chance to return the key for the filing cabinet with those records. Because of her he had a copy of Jonathon's birth certificate, and his name wasn't in the slot for father; no one's

75

name was. A circumstance which, he was happy to tell the first elder of Brianna's church when he showed him the birth certificate, could have been avoided if Brianna had told him about his child and let him see him. Tonight he would give Paula Hayward what she'd been hinting at with her body language since he got here, and if she wanted more…so be it. He always gave women what they wanted.

CHAPTER XIII

Jonathon was sitting on a chair in one corner of the lounge. With the plastic bag beneath his rear Brianna got the message. He'd had an accident.

"Hey, Jonathon," she said softly.

He didn't look up with his usual smile and eagerness at her voice. "I'm sorry," he said dully.

Bri knelt by his chair. "There's nothing to apologize for, Jon," she soothed, rubbing a hand across his back. "It was an accident."

"I called daddy. Mr. Hamilton gave me his phone. Daddy's phone is disconnected, mommy." He looked up then with tears in his eyes. "I-Is d-daddy coming back?"

Brianna's heart splintered, hurting at his pain, distraught at his distress, and helpless to do anything about it. What could she say? She didn't know where Bart was and didn't know if he was coming back. Like she had been doing since last night when he asked for his father, she switched the subject. "Let's get you changed first," she suggested.

Jon looked at her, his expression clearly communicating, *that's not what I asked you.* He stood slowly and took the plastic bag of clothing she offered. "I'll go change in the bathroom," he said. At the door he turned back and spoke, "I called daddy because I didn't want you to know; but he didn't answer, and he didn't come. Mr. Hamilton was very nice. He sent the kids that didn't go to gym to Mrs. Smith's class, so nobody would see that I was wet when I got up. He made sure the hallway was clear and took me to the teacher's lounge. It was empty too." He smiled—a sort of sad and pathetic shifting of his boyish lips. "He kept my secret just like daddy would. Do you think he could be my daddy if daddy doesn't come back?"

Apparently he didn't expect an answer because he walked out the door, leaving Brianna behind in a state of complete shock. She fell into the nearest chair. With her hands to her head, she stared at the Formica topped desk next to the chair. Oh, Bart, where are you? She wailed silently. He was worried about Christopher Hamilton stealing Jon's affection. Now by his absence he was enabling it. Bowing her head she prayed like never before, begging God to send her husband home and to fix the mess they had made of their lives.

***

That disgusting, fraud-faced scoundrel! Enemy turned empathizer my foot! All along Bart had been right about Christopher Hamilton. His peaceful, trust-me-I-mean-you-no-harm approach was a façade. Just like Bart suspected, that evil-doer was a wolf in sheep's clothing. Brianna sat in the pastor's study across from the First Elder of her church, simmering and trying to keep a lid on her anger.

"So, Elder Nolan, let me see if I understand this correctly. You are accusing me of withholding my child from his father, living in sin with Bart Roach, and you are basing all this on information from a stranger off the street, Christopher Hamilton?"

Elder Nolan regarded her coolly. "I'm not accusing you, Ms. Robinson. I'm just seeking to address with you some information that was brought to my attention last night."

"By some stranger whom you've never met and who might very well be lying," Brianna snapped sarcastically. "The man claims I left his name off my son's birth certificate deliberately. He told you my husband adopted his child, my child, improperly. Furthermore he claims that Bart and I aren't really married and he wants to remove his son from that immoral situation. And you didn't stop to think all this is far-fetched?" Nolan had never liked her. From the time she put him in his place for grabbing Jon by the collar as he was running in church, he'd been very cold towards her. Brianna had no problems with adults correcting her child. She had a heap of problems with them putting their hands on her son, and some of these church people didn't understand that you didn't have to poke, pinch, or grab children to make them behave.

"I never said I never met the man," he said, his tone hostile. "You're making an assumption, and those who do that make mules out of themselves."

Oh, no he didn't. He didn't just call her an ass. First Elder or not, Brianna would not let him get away with that. "It takes one jackass to know another," she shot back.

He actually looked shocked that she'd said that. What? He thought she would take his insults just because he was the First Elder? He'd better think again. *You earn my respect brother; it's not an entitlement.*

"You know what Ms. Robinson? I was prepared to give you the benefit of the doubt, but with your behavior now I don't think there's any doubt that this man's accusations against you have merit. If you conduct yourself in your personal affairs the way you just behaved in God's house, then I'm sure you're always at odds with people. When the pastor returns, I will be recommending your permanent removal from the praise team. I will also ask that Bart Roach not serve as deacon or play the drums until you both produce a marriage certificate. I always thought it strange for married people to have different names." He stood and pushed his chair back.

Brianna had given him time to finish because she wanted to confirm that he was personally prejudiced against her and that was his motivation for rushing to judgment. His last statement clinched her suspicion. She stood too. If he thought she would give him the last word, he was in for a surprise. She began the same way he had, "You know what, Elder? *You* were *not* prepared to give me the benefit of the doubt. What you just said proves that and confirms your personal dislike of me." He opened his mouth to object, and she shut him up straightaway. "Let me talk! I didn't interrupt you. I couldn't care less about your opinion of me. Feel free to make whatever recommendations to the pastor that you want. Remove me and my husband from church office. I really don't care. Unlike you we don't need positions to serve God. A church office doesn't give us identities like it does to *some*." If that pointed remark had flown over his head, Brianna's disparaging look and tone solidified the insult. He snapped more erect, and his lips which had been pinched before turned tighter with the affront.

Brianna did not care. He'd insulted her and had the gall when she retaliated to condemn her behavior in God's house? Sometimes she really disliked these hypocrites masquerading as followers of Christ. Give her the Babylonians any day. They didn't smoke, drink, and curse undercover. With them, what you see is what you get. With some of the church folk, they acted all righteous and holy on the outside while inside they were haters of their brothers like this one before her and

Christopher Hamilton too. Bri wrapped it up. She had wasted enough of her Friday evening. "As for Bart and I showing you a marriage certificate, you can go to hell!" Bri spun on her heel and marched out the door, leaving the First Elder behind catching flies at her final word choice.

She went to the Children's Ministry room to pull Jonathon out of choir practice. Agitated and upset by the hypocrisy and wickedness she'd just experienced, she hurried with her son to her car. The problems just seemed to keep piling up, and Bart still hadn't come home.

CHAPTER XIV

Bart stood outside his own front door, hesitating to go in. Brianna was home. Her car was parked in the driveway beside the house. Man up, you have to face her sometime. He roused his courage, squared his shoulders, and put the key in the lock. Her apartment door was open. He'd half-hoped it would be locked. Then he'd have had an excuse to creep upstairs and delay some more.

Not only was the door open, but she was standing in the living room, looking out the window into the street. She seemed very small and alone, standing there with her arms wrapped around her like she was cold. Seeing her after three days made him warm. He wanted to go over and wrap *his* arms around her and give her some of the heat she was generating in him.

He watched while her hands fell to her sides. She had something in her left hand. She held it up and slid her arms inside…his shirt. Bart's heart stumbled in surprise and started beating frantically with hope. Hatred towards him couldn't be her chief emotion now while she wore his shirt, could it? To know for sure, he put one foot forward to test the waters.

***

"Daddddddy!!!"

Bart swung his gaze right to see Jonathon barreling towards him, his arms outstretched in welcome and his face brighter than a hundred and twenty watt light bulb. He fell to his knees in time to catch the little boy as he flung himself into his arms.

"Daddy, I missed you," he declared. "I missed you sooooo much." Jon's voice wobbled. He stopped talking and just squeezed his arms tightly around his father's neck and pressed his small body against Bart's chest.

Overwhelmed with the level of love, Bart couldn't find words to say anything. Even if he had words, he wouldn't be able to speak. The intensity of his son's love, the depth of his affection, the profound admission that he missed him disabled Bart's vocal chords. He held his son, letting him know through the tightness of his embrace that he missed him and loved him too.

"I needed you on Friday, and you weren't there," Jon complained at a whisper.

"Sorry, buddy. Why'd you need me?" Bart whispered back not knowing why they were speaking in low tones.

"I had an accident," he mumbled, burrowing his face in Bart's neck.

"Oh, Jon," Bart murmured sympathetically, running his hand over the boy's head. He needed a hair cut again.

"I called you and they said your phone wasn't working," Jon continued.

"I lost it and stopped the service until I could get it replaced."

"I thought you'd gone forever."

Bart squeezed him tighter. "I'd never do that to you Jon. I

love you too much."

"I love you too, Daddy. I love you very, very much."

Bart figured that with the way Jon was attached to him like a second layer of skin, he couldn't disengage himself to go and greet Brianna. He pushed to his feet, cradling the child to his chest with one hand. Shifting Jon's weight to his left side he turned to face the now vacant window. Where had Bri gone? He hadn't seen her move. Well for some brief moments he'd had his eyes closed while hugging Jonathon. Maybe she left the room then. Would she answer him if he called out? Could he venture any further into her space? The last time he was here, she'd told him not to come back. The way he'd left erased his chances of acquiring an invitation back into her space or into her heart. But she was wearing your shirt, he reminded himself, bolstering his spirit with that image. Had she gotten the written apology he'd FedExed to her?

"Where's mommy?" Jon asked, twisting in Bart's arms and looking around. "Mommy!" he shouted. "Daddy's home."

Bart ventured as far as the wide archway, leading from the living room into the dining room.

Brianna emerged from the back of the apartment. She stopped on the other side of the dining table. She wasn't wearing his shirt now. His heart did a free fall–kind of like going bungee jumping without a rope. How should he read that? She's done with you? How else, you idiot? Bart's chest felt suddenly tight. He shifted Jon's weight so he could breathe better. Nobody spoke. When he looked at Brianna, her gaze shifted to some point of focus other than him. When she looked at him, he did the same. Jon glanced from one to the other, his youthful face troubled. Tension silently permeated the air like a noxious gas, slowly tainting the atmosphere and making the occupants in the room uneasy.

Knowing something had to give, and trying to avoid losing his mind, Bart broke the quiet. "Hi, Bri."

The two words fell into the vacuum of silence, sounding and feeling inadequate to span the unbridgeable distance between him and the woman whom he loved but whom he was finding it hard to even talk to.

"Hi." Her gaze jumped to his and away lightning-bolt fast. Her jerky smile appeared and disappeared at the same pace.

This had gone beyond awkward. Maybe if they were alone. "Jon, buddy, can you go to your room for a bit?"

"No," the child protested, shaking his head vehemently and holding on tightly when Bart tried to put him down.

"I need to talk to mommy alone," he whispered, hoping Brianna couldn't hear.

Jonathon still shook his head. "The last time you sent me to my room, you and mommy had a big fight. You disappeared and she can't stop crying."

"Jon!"

Bart turned his attention to Brianna at her outburst of embarrassment. She'd been crying since he left? Was it because of what he'd done or because he hadn't come home? Despair battled hope inside his chest and neither one was winning. While that war raged, he made a decision—two actually. He had to get Brianna out of the house and Jon to a babysitter. He wanted to talk to her on neutral ground rather than in the apartment where memories of his treatment on Thursday might still be lingering. He couldn't say what needed to be said in front of his son, so he hoped to God Julia and John were home today because he was about to dump his child on them for a few hours. Of course all this hinged on getting Bri to come with him. He cleared his throat, "You know, I haven't eaten yet, and hope you haven't either." He glanced at his watch:

Three o'clock. They usually cooked and ate dinner later on Sundays. On the Sundays she didn't work, Bri rarely started dinner before four. "Why don't we go out to eat?"

"Yes!" Jon was immediately in agreement. "Put me down so that I can get my shoes and coat." He started wiggling to get down.

Bart put him down, and the boy ran off to get his things. Bart started talking as soon as he disappeared, knowing he'd be back too quickly to say everything. "Bri, I understand if you don't want to go, but I thought if w—"

"Mom wanted Jon to come over and play with Ruth-Ann and the kids," she interrupted him. Ruth-Ann and her brothers were Jonathon's aunt and uncles. It was interesting that he was older than they were. Julia, Brianna's mom, had remarried and started a family with Bart's brother, John, when Bri was twenty years old.

God's hand had to be in this, Bart thought. He'd been planning to leave Jonathon with Julia and John.

"I agreed to bring him over at four thirty; so he can't go out to dinner. Mom already cooked and wants him to eat over there."

Bart's heart skipped a beat. She just said 'he can't go.' What did that mean? That she wasn't including herself in the dinner invitation? "Will you?" he asked, weary with the doubt.

"Will I what?" She asked in confusion.

"Go to dinner."

Her expression shifted to uncertain. "If the invitation includes me, then yes," she answered slowly.

Bart thought he'd been pretty clear when he issued the invitation, but with things unresolved between them, he would bet she was feeling as unsure around him as he was around her.

"Yes it does," he said.

Jon ran back into the room then with his sneakers and his coat on. "I'm ready to go to grandma's," he announced. Both Bri and Bart looked down at him in surprise. He grinned up at them. "I was listening," he admitted shamelessly. "Playing with Ruth-Ann, Little John, and Josiah is more fun that going to a restaurant with you and mommy." He made an endearing face and added, "Sorry. I still love you." His parents laughed.

CHAPTER XV

As Bart navigated the Sunday evening traffic going east into Long Island, Brianna prayed for forgiveness. Her mother hadn't been expecting Jonathon to come over. No play date had been set up with his aunt and uncles. But she had to find a way to talk to Bart in private and her only solution was getting Jonathon a babysitter. She knew her mother wouldn't refuse to keep him. Besides, yesterday she had poured out the whole story to her mother and given her permission to share the details with her husband. Julia had been shocked that Bri had been married all this time and hadn't told her. But she got over that and listened in empathy as Bri expressed how much she wanted to save her marriage that up to now had been in name only, a condition which she desperately wanted to change. She needed to get her husband back to do that though.

So when she texted Julia en route to her house in Westbury, Bri wasn't surprised to see a reply text saying: *Hallelujah! Bring Jon now. Good luck. John and I r praying 4 u guys.*

***

Henry's, a popular West Indian restaurant in Queens, New York, was nearly at capacity on this Sunday evening. There wasn't a day when the place wasn't packed. Serving authentic Jamaican Jerked Chicken and Curried Goat, the restaurant was heavily patronized by Jamaican nationals as well a multiplicity of other islanders and many others who got hooked on the place with just a taste or as the Jamaican's would say *jus' a tase*. With the menu expanded to include vegetarian dishes, the restaurant significantly increased its customer base. Bri's dishes of choice were the Stir Fried Tofu and Tofu Run Down, a succulent dish traditionally made with mackerel, coconut milk and seasoned with herbs and spices. The tofu substituted the mackerel, and the dish tasted just as delicious to Bri.

Apparently Bart had called ahead because the hostess ushered them to their seats as soon as he gave his name. The woman led them to a corner table for two at the western side of the restaurant. With the muted lighting and the lowered window shades, the atmosphere was intimate. The seating on this side of the restaurant seemed to have been created with privacy in mind what with the greater distance of tables from each other. All the seating on this side was also for couples.

Bart picked up his menu and glanced at it. Bri didn't touch hers. She knew what she wanted: Stir fried tofu with rice and peas. Bri glanced around. The decor of the place had been updated recently. The lower portion of the wall now sported imitation bamboo shoots, varnished to a toffee-colored shine. The upper portion, separated from the lower by a thin layer of carved wood, was painted in a muted shade of green edging into aqua. They'd kept the mini coconut trees, which were really miniature lamps, on each table.

Running out of places to cast her gaze, she turned her eyes upon her husband still studying his menu. They ate here frequently enough for him not to need it, so she had no clue what he was searching so diligently for. Unless like her he was searching for a way to shatter this seemingly unbreakable silence between them. There was much to be said and a great deal of acrimony hanging in the air that needed clearance, but how did one begin? And who should take the lead? He asked her out. Bri hoped he'd take the initiative because she didn't really know how to make up. In all the years they had been together as friends, they hadn't had a major quarrel. Differences of opinion had occurred but in retrospect, more often than not, Bart had yielded to her opinion. Today, for the first time, she acknowledged to herself that she had taken him for granted. He was nice, even tempered, understanding, and always accommodating. She never thought he had it in him to blow like he had last Thursday. It wasn't a side of him she ever wanted to see again.

"Bart," she began.

He looked up and set aside his menu as soon as she called his name. Now that his blue eyes were focused directly on her, searching, intense, and saturated with longing, Bri forgot what she wanted to say and paused.

The waitress came just then and took their order, unwittingly filling the sudden silence. He ordered what she did.

"You were saying?" he prompted her when the woman walked away.

Brianna laughed a little. "I wasn't saying anything, at least not yet. I'm just trying to get my thoughts together to say what I need to in the right way," she admitted.

He rested his elbow on the table and propped his chin in his palm. "That's funny. I'm trying to do the same thing."

"Really?"

He nodded.

"Since when did we start doing that? We never had a problem communicating before." That was true. Conversation between them had always been easy. Differences never escalated to deep disagreements to the point of them becoming uncomfortable with each other like now.

"Since I was stupid enough to say the wrong thing and do something even worse, I think I'd better go first." He broke eye contact when he said it and shifted back in his chair, clearly uncomfortable. "I want to apologize but every word I think of sounds inadequate. I want to tell you I'm sorry and that I regret what I said and did, but I know it can't erase the words and the deed. I feel like you deserve better." He met her eyes then, his full of the regret and sorrow he thought insufficient. "I'm sorry, Bri for all of it. For every word I spoke to diminish you and the beautiful person that you are, I apologize. For the way I touched you." He stopped as she flinched. Bri watched his mouth go tight at her reaction, but she couldn't help it because the image was in her head and it wasn't pretty. "It was disrespectful and insulting and it shouldn't have happened." He took a deep breath. "I know my bringing it up is difficult for you. It is for me." He dropped his gaze and shifted in his chair once more. "I want you to know you have nothing to fear from me ever again. I promise I won't ever touch you again."

Brianna kept her focus on the table cloth. Her mind snagged on his last words and refused to release them. They kept playing in her head like a jammed CD. *I won't ever touch you again.* They sounded ominous, final, and totally irreversible. Bri's problem was that she wanted his touch, not the last one she'd experienced, but the one she'd experienced in the kiss last Thursday morning, and in their first kiss two years ago. Those touches had been fleeting and tantalizing, leaving her yearning for the fulfillment she knew existed beyond those surface caresses. She had to find a way to tell Bart that. "I can't accept that," she said softly.

"I'm sorry?"

"No, I'm sorry." She knew he was asking for clarification of her previous statement, but it was way past time for her to apologize. He wasn't the only one at fault here. "I took you for granted. I presumed that you would understand about Christopher. I expected you to because you are Bart. You're the man who gave me everything I wanted. It never entered my head that I'd be making you insecure with Jon's love by telling you what I did about Christopher on Wednesday. I never gave you any assurance that I cared." Bri stopped. About to make the biggest admission of her life, she wanted him to understand that she was giving him her whole self with her next words. "Bart, I l—"

"Ms. Robinson. What a surprise."

Never interrupt a woman and especially not a woman confessing her undying love to her man. It didn't help that the intruder was at the top of Bri's hit list. Brianna gave Christopher Hamilton a look that could have dynamited a weapon of mass destruction. This snake, this sewer reject had been slithering around, pretending to be reformed on the surface while beneath he was the same old worthless, good for nothing excuse for a human being, wreaking havoc in people's lives. His latest mischief being the lies he'd told the First Elder and the consequences of same surged to the forefront of Brianna's brain. Brianna felt her anger soar as he stood there grinning. And then he fueled the flame in her to an almost out-of-control burn when he had the temerity to turn to a curious Bart and introduce himself. Bart's smile faded as soon as he said his name.

"This table is occupied, and you're making my air impure by being here. Get lost!" She didn't raise her voice, but the words flew through her teeth like darts.

He started to turn to her again.

"You heard my wife. Move on." Bart's order came out low and quiet, but Bri heard a bite in his voice that she'd never heard before.

"Your wife?" Christopher said scornfully. "She gave it to me for free y—"

Bart backhanded him so hard, Christopher did a one—eighty before crashing into a nearby table some occupants had just vacated. Somebody cursed; people scattered. Christopher pushed off the table that had broken his fall. When he turned to face them, his mouth was bleeding and his eyes were full of hatred. "You'll pay for this. Both of you will pay for this," he mumbled through injured lips.

"What is going on here?" Henry arrived with two body builder types, obviously security. He looked from Bart to Brianna. He knew them and the entire Roach family. They patronized his restaurant a lot.

"This man attacked me," Christopher pointed an accusing finger at Bart.

"Mr. Roach?" Henry inquired.

"Bri and I just came in for dinner, Henry. This guy interrupted our meal. We told him to leave our table. He disrespected my wife. I paid him back for that." Bart shrugged like it was no big deal.

"I didn't hit her. You hit me!" Christopher exclaimed.

"If you had, I'd have done more than hit you," Bart spoke quietly, giving the man a cool look.

"I'm sorry, Mr. Roach," Henry addressed Bart apologetically, "I'm going to have to ask you to leave. It's restaurant policy to ask any patron in an altercation to vacate the premises."

Bart nodded in understanding. "I know, Henry. Bri and I

were leaving anyway. I'll take care of the meal on the way out."

"No, please, Mr. Roach. From what I can see you haven't even gotten your dinner yet. It's on the house."

"Thanks, Henry." He smiled at the man. "Bri, are you ready to leave?" he asked.

More than ready to go, she nodded, put on her coat and moved ahead of him to the door.

Behind them, Bri heard Henry tell security to "Help this gentleman to the door."

"Why didn't you escort them?" she heard Christopher protest.

"We reserve this service exclusively for you," Henry said, his tone dripping with sarcasm.

CHAPTER XVI

Outside, the warmth, following yesterday's twenty degree plus temperature, was a precursor of the snow to come. The meteorologists had been playing with the figures. First six to eight inches were expected. The last report she'd heard said two to four inches to Jonathon's disappointment. He'd been hoping for a snow day. Bri let her coat hang open as they walked across the parking lot to the Jeep. Bart was back to being quiet, and she didn't know how to resume the conversation that Christopher had interrupted. She couldn't blurt out 'I love you,' could she? That was a declaration that you built up to.

At the Sports Utility vehicle, he opened her door and walked around the hood to the driver's side. Bart whispered a prayer and pulled out of the lot. It was a short ride to the house. He pulled into the driveway, and they got down.

At the front door, Brianna felt his presence behind her. She thought she heard him sigh. With what? Regret at how the evening had turned out? She regretted the way it had ended too. Her thoughts occupied by more than the opening of the door, she fumbled with the key in the lock. Her hand stilled, her body went motionless, and her breathing ceased when Bart's bigger hand closed over hers. Together they unlocked the door. Did unlocking the door of their house together symbolize them unlocking the door to their future? She certainly hoped so.

***

He'd promised not to touch her, but she couldn't get the door open. He had just lent assistance. But the softness of her hand reminded Bart of why he liked touching Bri and the smoothness of her skin made him yearn to slide his hands over other silken areas of her body. She stepped inside and he followed her in, closing the front door behind him.

At the door of her apartment, she turned to face him, her manner hesitant. "I'm sorry the dinner turned out badly."

Bart shrugged. He was sorry too, but there was nothing they could do now to recover the moment when she'd been about to declare something monumental, going by the expression that had been in her eyes. "It's okay."

She was twisting the keys in her hands now. Nervousness. "Maybe if I hadn't gone off on him none of this would have happened."

"It's not your fault, Bri. He should have left when you told him to," Bart reassured her.

"He made me angry coming over to our table as if we were friends after what he did."

Christopher Hamilton had done something to Bri? Bart felt an adrenalin surge. What had that man done to his woman? "What did he do to you?" He was glad the question came out calm. He wasn't feeling tranquil at all.

She explained about what he'd told the first elder and that man's subsequent reaction.

"I'd have hit him more than once if I'd known," Bart said, folding and unfolding his fists, wishing now that he'd indeed hit Christopher Hamilton again or at least a little harder. He didn't want that man teaching his child any more.

Brianna could see that discussing Christopher Hamilton was getting Bart upset. She didn't want Christopher to be the focus of tonight. He'd already disrupted their lives enough. To move Bart's mind from the man and also bring him to a place where they could finish the conversation that they started in the restaurant, she offered, "Do you want to come in? I can fix us something to eat—a sandwich, some cereal, a fruit bowl?"

Bart ran his hand over his head in frustration. He didn't want any food. What he wanted he couldn't have—her.

"No thanks, Bri. It's late and we have work tomorrow."

***

It was seven o'clock for goodness sake. How was that late? An uneasy feeling started growing in the pit of her stomach. Was he trying to avoid her? Had he been serious earlier about never, ever touching her again? Had he lost the interest he'd had all this time, and so quickly? Had those harmful words she said to him turned him off her for good? But he'd hit Christopher because the man had made a derogatory comment about her. Maybe he still cared. He had to care to have reacted with the emotional violence that he had.

She didn't want to be in her apartment or her bed alone tonight, but with her husband's reticence in accepting her invitation to come in, it looked like she was going to be alone. At least she had Jonathon. Jonathon! Brianna slapped her forehead, remembering her son. She had to pick him up from her mother's place. Turning towards the front door she said, "I have to get Jon from mom's. He has school tomorrow."

"Bri, get him in the morning."

"It's not late," she objected, reaching of the handle of the front door. "I can go now."

"Don't go," he said and added "please."

"Give me a reason to stay," she whispered, not believing that she had said that.

"It's standing right behind you." He was nearer; his voice was closer. His cadence had dipped from normal husky to deep sexy. The air in the hallway started thinning out, and she struggled to take even breaths.

Brianna turned slowly to face the man whom she'd flirted with these many years, confided in for so long, kept as a friend all this time, married for years, and whom she now and for a long time wanted as a real husband. Her heartbeat shifted gears into overdrive. She took a step forward to claim what she wanted. He stepped backwards. By his third act of retreat, Brianna was confused. He helped her to understand.

"I'm not invincible," he said.

Brianna still didn't comprehend.

"I made you a promise tonight that I can't keep," he explained. "I said I'd never touch you again, but honestly, Brianna, I don't want to keep it." He stopped backing up at the bottom of the stairs. She stopped less than the length of an arm away. "I think the million dollar question is, do you want me to keep it?"

Bri needed no clarification on his meaning now. She shook her head slowly. "No, I don't want you to." She smiled at him, a genuine and free smile and the first of its kind since he'd come home.

"I guess we're on the same page then," he murmured huskily, reaching for her, wrapping his fingers lightly around her arm and tugging her closer. Bri went willingly. And then she remembered what she hadn't finished telling him. She flattened her palms on his chest. He felt so solid and wonderful and male. Bri caught her floating thoughts and focused on what she needed to say. "At Henry's I started to tell you that I...that

I..." Communication had never been so challenging. She wanted to say all that had been in her heart for a long time. "I love you" alone seemed insufficient. Brianna curled her fingers into the fabric of his shirt as she struggled to articulate the fullness of her emotions.

He pulled her fully against his chest and wrapped his arms around her. Bri relaxed, sighing the sound of fulfillment, the feeling of finally reaching home, and being in a place where she always wanted to be—a happy place, a peaceful place, and a loving one. She felt all that and experienced all that in the arms of this man. "I've admired you from the time that I met you," she confessed, tipping her head back to meet his eyes. "There have been times where I wondered how I could be so blessed to have met someone as wonderful as you."

The corner of his mouth kicked up slightly at that admission. He leaned forward and brushed his lips across her forehead. "I think you're amazing too," he murmured.

Bri smiled and rested her cheek on his shoulder. "You've always, always been there for me and Jonathon. I've been very needy these past seven years of our friendship; yet you never grew tired of meeting those needs. You met them when I asked you and when I didn't ask. I remember thinking one time, is this guy for real? Does his generosity ever run out? Will it ever? Not that I wanted it to." She looked up with seriousness so he could get that she was sober. "I've been selfish with you Bart, inconsiderate of your needs." She laid a finger against his lips when he tried to interrupt her. "No, shush, let me finish. I'm going somewhere with this." Bri let her fingers wander over his chin. She pressed her forefinger slightly into the cleft of it and moved her hand to cup his jaw, strong and solid like the man and his character. "I've monopolized your time these last seven years with scant consideration that you had a life or could have a life outside of me and Jonathon. On Thursday, my co-worker, Tanya, told me what I'd done to you was a bad thing and I needed to stop.

"Well Tanya had a point, but I'm not going to apologize for taking up your time because I'd be lying if I said I regretted it. If I had to do it all over again I'd do the same thing. I figured that if all of your focus was on me and on Jonathon then you wouldn't have time to look at another woman, to wander away, to think of another family—of forming another family. And I hoped that if we spent much time together, you would grow to love me as much as I love you."

He didn't say anything for several moments, but the tightness of his hold and the way his Adams apple kept sliding up and down told Brianna a lot about the state of his emotions. "You." His voice sounded scrub-brush-on-washboard rough. He stopped and cleared his throat. "You love me?" He asked, his question filled with awe. The hushed quality of it spoke of incredulity.

She met his blue gaze, sparkling now with the dawning of belief and the fullness of joy. "I love you, Bartholomew Roach," she said, enunciating her words so that her meaning could not be mistaken.

He cupped her cheeks and let his eyes roam over her face. Bri let him, her smile lengthening with joy at the love that his expression broadcasted, and it was all hers. "Do you know how long I've been waiting for you to say that?" he asked.

"Do you know how long I've wanted to say that," she came back, laughing.

He wrapped his arms more tightly around her, kissed her on the nose and on her cheek. Brianna wondered when he was going to get to her mouth. "When did you first know that you loved me?" he asked, resting his chin atop her head.

"Do you remember when Jon got a stomach virus four years ago and the doctor had to check his blood?"

"I remember."

"Remember how he screamed and wouldn't keep still for them to take the blood until you let them pull your blood too while they did his so he could see there was nothing to it?"

Bart chuckled. "I remember that. He screamed until his voice broke. He knew I was scared of needles. I figured if I let them stick me too, being afraid, he'd find the strength to do it also."

"That's when I fell in love with you."

"Really?" He tucked his chin and looked at her in a 'that's all it took' type of way. "If I'd known that's all I needed to do to win your love, I'd have arranged a blood draw with Jon's pediatrician a long time ago."

"Bart you're so idiotic," Brianna laughed.

"But you love me and that's all I care about." He squeezed her close and kissed her.

That's all she cared about too. She ran her hand over his bicep. "When did *you* first know that you loved me?"

"The night Jon was born. The nurse handed him to you and said 'here's your baby.' You turned to me and said, 'Look at our baby.' That's when I knew that a future without you and Jon wasn't possible because I cared about you too much to live without you. I knew I loved you then, Brianna. He looked down at her. "Hey!" he said when her eyes glistened. "I didn't say that to make you cry."

"I know," she sniffed. "But I can't help it. It's so touching and wonderful, and it makes me so happy that I cry."

Bart laughed. Girls. Go figure. They cried when they were happy. What did they do when they were sad? The opposite more than likely.

There was something she should tell him since they seemed to be bringing things out into the open. But the hallway wasn't the place to share it. "Come," she said, pushing out his arms and unlocking her front door.

Bri walked into her living room and plopped her purse on the central table. She dropped unto the sofa and patted the space beside her, inviting Bart to sit. He was half-way seated when he snapped his fingers and said, "Oh, I forgot one thing. I'll be right back." He ran out of the apartment, leaving Brianna behind in bewilderment. She heard his footsteps pounding up the stairs.

He returned at a more sedate pace and when he came through the door, she understood why. In one hand he held a basket floral arrangement, the variety in it so diverse that Bri couldn't identify all of the flowers. In his right hand he held a single, long-stemmed red rose. Bart stopped before her. She rose from the sofa awed and extremely curious. When had he bought these?

"This is for you." He offered her the single stemmed rose. You should have gotten that yesterday via delivery but because it was the Sabbath I couldn't have it delivered. So instead, I personally brought it to you."

"Thank you, Bart." She inhaled the sweetness of the flower. "It is beautiful."

"You are beautiful and the occasion is my second apology for the awful words I said and for what I did to you."

"Your second apology?" Brianna raised her eyebrows while he grimaced.

"I take it you didn't get a FedEx package from me."

"Oh, that's the FedEx envelope Tanya texted me about yesterday. "You sent it to my job?"

"I did. I sent it overnight on Friday. I thought you were going in today and would pick it up then."

"It's my Sunday off. What's in the package?"

"A card with an apology. My own words from my heart."

"If they were anything like your earlier one at the restaurant, moving and sincere, then I accept that apology too."

"Thank you, Bri. That means a lot," he said, his blue eyes genuine.

What else could she do? She loved him. She smiled and gestured at the bouquet. "And this one?"

"This one is being delivered on schedule. The plan was if you didn't reject the two previous deliveries, then it would be safe for me to bring this in person and tell you how sorry I am." He swallowed. "I am so sorry, Brianna. Will you forgive me?"

She took the basket from him, held it close, and inhaled the perfume from the varying petals. Setting the bouquet on the table, she kissed Bart's cheek, took his hand and pulled him down unto the sofa beside her. "I forgive you," she said softly, scooting into the curve of his open arm and snuggling up to his side.

He curved his arm around her shoulder and pulled her closer. "I was so afraid you wanted a divorce," he revealed his fear.

Brianna ran her hand along his thigh. "I was angry and hurt. I wanted to make you feel some of my pain. It was a stupid thing to say. I didn't mean it. And I didn't mean all that foolishness about being interested in Christopher. Again it was meant to hurt you because you hurt me by what you said." She looked up at him. "It was stupid, and I almost lost you. I'm glad I didn't and I'm sorry for all the terrible things I said to you."

He kissed her, a fleeting brush of his mouth across hers.

Brianna wanted so much more.

"I have a secret," she announced softly.

His fingers curved tighter, an almost imperceptible movement, and then he relaxed his hand. "I'm listening, " he said.

Brianna bit her lip. "Two secrets actually."

"What are they?" he encouraged.

Brianna found his gaze curious rather than suspicious when she looked up. She breathed a little easier.

"I want more than a paper marriage," she admitted.

***

Bart went very still. He'd anticipated that her declaration of love meant this, but it still stunned him to hear her admit it. Euphoria replaced shock faster than a 1-2-3 count. He glanced down at Bri. She had her head bowed and appeared to be studying her finger nails. Had she turned shy after that bold admission? He leaned down and grazed her ear with his lips.

She raised her shoulder to her ear and giggled. "That tickles," she mumbled.

"Maybe I didn't do it right," he offered and repeated it.

"One more time."

He met her demand. Only this time she shifted her head so that his lips grazed her cheek and stopped just a tad shy of the left corner of her lips. He kissed the corner and watched her lips part slightly to release a tiny moan of pleasure, not the full blown kind but more like the embers of one. That small sound stoked the low fires of need that had been burning forever inside of him. When she shifted and offered, "Last one," in a low, husky, and seductive tone, Bart didn't need another invitation. He closed the distance to her mouth with a mere movement of his. It was like sinking into cotton candy. Soft and delicious, her lips tasted like sugar and gave him the same rush. Bart's heart jumped and began pumping more blood per second than it normally did. His body thrummed with want, and a need climbed in him to kiss her deeper, bring her closer, and touch her more intimately than a brush of his fingers across her arm. He ran his fingers through her hair, enjoying the soft, silky feel of the black curtain sliding across his palm. He touched her cheek with his free hand, letting his hand glide south until it rested on her chest. He heard her breathing quicken beneath the kiss and increased the pressure of his lips against hers. Her eager response stoked the yearning in him to push boundaries that had never been tested before and break barriers that had never been breached with Bri until now.

He kissed her long and strong and slow, letting her feel his need, making her enjoy what he offered, leaving her wanting more. And when she whimpered for more, Bart took intensity to explosive, breaching the barrier of her lips, claiming her warmth within, showing her how profoundly a husband and wife could connect with one another. When he pulled back he was breathing hard. Brianna reclined in the curve of his arm, looking spacey and replete. Bart let his gaze travel over her face, proud that he'd put that contented expression on it. She was beautiful, she loved him, and she was his wife. He considered himself blessed. He watched her bosom rise and fall beneath powder pink cashmere. The tiny, pearl-like buttons down the front strained to hold the garment together as the fullness of her bosom tested their determination to uphold her modesty. Bart felt tempted to help them lose the battle. His fingers were less than an inch away from putting thought to action when Bri spoke, "I want more."

Bart was on board with that. He wanted much more too.

"I want more of this and more than this." She lifted her lashes to reveal passion rich eyes.

Bart swallowed, shaken by the depth of need in her gaze. If one kiss had done that, he could only imagine that it was going to be a long and wonderful night with his wife.

***

Brianna lowered her lashes and tried to even out her accelerated breathing. The way Bart watched her with that heavy, hungry gaze sent a clear message that the time for talking had expired. Tonight, in fact right now, they were going somewhere they had never been together before. But first she needed to tell him why she'd taken so long to be his wife in full. The reason hinged on the two secrets she'd mentioned before. "Remember the secrets I spoke about earlier," she began.

He nodded but slowly like it took effort to follow her conversation. With the intense and intimate look he kept sliding over her person, she imagined there was only one thing on his mind right now.

"Well the first one is I didn't want to invest emotionally in any relationship again, not after the first disaster. That's one of the reasons it took so long for me to admit even to myself that I loved you."

"And the second one?"

"Bart, my first time wasn't good," Brianna blurted.

"Your first time?" he echoed. After a moment of silence from her he said, 'oh', softly. Another followed that, a longer sound of total understanding. "Bri, Bri, I'm so sorry."

"That's why it took so long for me to-to get to this place with you." She closed her eyes. "It was hot and sweaty and quick—totally unsatisfying."

***

Oh, God. Bart closed his eyes, sensing the night with his wife slipping out of his grasp. "Bri, we don't have to do this, at least not tonight." Bart felt like he'd just cut off his arm. He

106

wanted to make love with his wife, had dreamed of it too many times to count, but if Bri came into this with bad memories, it wasn't going to work. And with his stupidity last Thursday, he might have added to those memories. He barely held in the groan of frustration swelling in his throat.

***

Brianna watched Bart fight disappointment and lose. He thought she didn't want them to be together, but that wasn't so. The way he made her feel just now with only a kiss, granted a very thorough, none-she-had-ever-experienced-before type of kiss, gave her confidence that everything else was going to be beautiful. Leaning down, she unzipped her boots and toed them off. Folding her legs beneath her, she faced him sideways. She shifted closer and kissed Bart on the cheek. "I want this tonight," she declared, feeling her face turning warm, and knowing that she was blushing. "I only told you my secrets so you could understand why I waited so long. I'm over that bad experience. With you, I know it's going to be beautiful. I want you, Bart."

He raised a doubtful eyebrow. "You're sure?""

"Positive."

His blue eyes changed hue as they had numerous times before when awareness permeated the air and when desire sparked and deepened, pretty much like now. He tugged her unto his lap and settled her against his chest. "Because once we start, there's no turning back. You know that right?"

"I know that," she managed around suddenly laden respirations, as her husband's hand slid under her sweater. Her stomach muscles tightened when his palm spread over her abdomen.

"Relax Bri." His smile said trust me, and because she did she obeyed him. "That's my girl," he praised her when he felt her tension ease. He leaned in and gave her a long, carnal kiss. He raised his head. "You shared two secrets with me so I'll share two with you. In fact, let me just show you." He scooted off the sofa with her in his arms.

"What?" Bri asked in confusion as he carried her to the back of the apartment.

"That was one secret," he revealed as he entered her bedroom. "I carried my bride over the threshold."

Brianna laughed, and temporarily forgot the worry in her mind about what lay ahead and of being unaware of what to do. "What's the other?" she asked as he placed her in the middle of the bed and climbed on beside her.

"This," he said, reaching out and resting his hand on her breast. "May I?" he asked, tugging at the top button of her cashmere sweater.

Brianna glanced down and blushed as she took his meaning. He wanted to undress her. "Yes," she told him, two seconds behind him undoing the first button.

"Feel free to return the favor," he invited, pausing in his task to take her hand and place it against the cotton shirt that covered his chest. "That's my second secret. It's kind of like a hidden fantasy. I figured that if the first couple, Adam and Eve, were naked and not ashamed, this clothing thing, nightgowns, pajamas, negligees were all overrated. I promised myself the first order of business on my wedding night would be to get rid of the barriers between us."

The matter-of-fact and humorous way he explained his secret made Brianna laugh and relaxed her. Not feeling shy anymore she went to work on the buttons of his shirt.

"I have another fantasy," he confessed.

Brianna glanced up from a very pleasurable exploration of his chest and followed his heavy lidded gaze to her now exposed bosom.

"This," he said and laid his head carefully in the valley between her breasts. "Hummmm. Now I'm content. This is home," he murmured.

Bri cradled his head to her bosom. She couldn't agree more. This was home—them together and like this.

CHAPTER XVII

Two days later

Christopher Hamilton walked into the school library with a professional smile that was fighting not to become a smirk on his face. The confident stride that carried him into the room turned into a confused stumble as the man whom he had thought was Bart Roach turned around. This wasn't Bart. It was that white guy, Brianna's father who'd stood toe to toe with his dad on that day years ago when Brianna said she was pregnant by him. He and his parents had denied it. His gaze shifted left to the three other occupants of the room whom he just now noticed. One looked like Brianna's dad and the other had enough resemblance to her dad for Christopher to peg him as the grandfather. He didn't know the tall black guy .

The door clicked closed behind him. Christopher spun, startled to face a short, stocky unsmiling black guy who looked enough like the other African-American man in the room for them to be related. Who were these people?

"Hey!" He shouted, grabbing for his phone that the stocky guy snatched from his shirt pocket. The man held the phone out of reach when he tried to grab it again. "Stop that!" the guy warned sharply, powering off the phone.

Christopher seethed. He'd had the phone on record. He'd planned to capture his conversation with Jonathon's father and to have on record any threat that the man might level against him. When the school's secretary had said Mr. Roach was here to see him, he thought Bart Roach had come to speak to him about what happened in the restaurant on Sunday. He'd been ready to goad the man into becoming angry and hoped to push him into threatening him. Then he would have a case against him. "Who are you people?" he demanded of the men in the quiet room. "I came here to speak with Mr. Roach."

Brianna's father smiled a slow predatory type of smile, or so Christopher thought. Seven years ago it made him uneasy. Now it chilled him. "I'm Mr. Roach and so are they," he said. "You should have asked which one before you came in here."

"Where is Bart Roach? If he didn't come to see me, then I'm leaving." He turned to exit, but the stocky guy blocked the door and the three to the left started closing in on him. He shifted to the right, real fear turning his body clammy with sweat. "What do you want?" His voice wasn't as steady as he would have liked.

"Just to talk," Brianna's dad said. "Have a seat. I'm getting a crick in my neck looking up at you."

"I prefer to stand," Christopher said coldly, glaring at the man whom he still detested after all this time. In that stand-off in the guidance counselor's office, Ms. Marsh had been the counselor's name, this man had torn him and his parents up. He had made them feel like persecutors of young women just because his daughter, Brianna, had been stupid enough to have unprotected sex and get caught carrying the result. And he was the one who'd brought up his past indiscretion in Maryland with

Selena Myers. The man had also threatened to tell the people of Patmos SAB Church about his promiscuous history. He and his daughter had gone further and done it, because he never got that job.

"Sit," the brawny guy at the door commanded, pulling out a chair. When he didn't obey, the guy who looked like Brianna's dad, not the old guy, stepped closer and began to tell him about the various ways you could hurt a person without leaving a bruise. Christopher didn't know if he was bluffing; but with the size of the man's hands, he didn't want to take a chance. He sat.

"Now," Brianna's dad started, his tone even but his unsmiling face far from friendly. "It's come to my attention that you've been disrupting my daughter's life again and threatening her family."

"Whoever said that is a liar," Christopher ground out.

"You're quick to point fingers, but that thumb leads right back to you. So I think you're the liar."

"I don't care what you think. I'm telling you somebody's accusing me falsely."

"And I don't care what you say," her dad shot back, his voice steely. "You are a menace to women, and it's going to stop right here and right now. You're not going to bother Brianna again."

"And just how do you think you can stop me?" he snarled scornfully. Who did these people think they were, coming in here and trying to intimidate him? He wasn't finished with Brianna Robinson until he decided he was.

Brianna's father smiled that unpleasant smile again. Christopher felt a drop of sweat trickle down his back. "You know guys," her dad addressed the other men in the room. "I was kind of hoping he'd ask that." Standing suddenly, he got right up in Christopher's face, "Listen you piece of crap, you've got a history of promiscuity so long that if it were a crime, you'd get capital punishment." He straightened up. "Now, since it seems you've forgotten, remember that job you didn't get with Mid-America? I arranged that."

Christopher flew from his seat, but when Brianna's dad stood his ground and the other men closed ranks around him, he sat back down easy as you please.

"And I'm prepared to make the same thing happen with this job," her father went on. "Do you think I don't know why you got fired from the Central South conference?"

Christopher's heart misfired. That evidence was sealed. Wasn't it? President Washington wouldn't share that with anyone, would he? He had taken the credentials. That had been enough, right? But Christopher wasn't sure at all.

"All it takes is one little word in the ear of your principal, Mrs. Garner, about the mess you left in Central South and you'll be history. Maybe you'd have hope and a prayer if you didn't teach Bible. But those imparting knowledge to our children, especially as it relates to God's word, must have upstanding moral characters. It clearly says that in the Teacher's Education Handbook. How interesting it would be if it were to leak out that the Bible teacher is a womanizer, a fornicator, and a hater of women."

"That last one is a lie," he shouted.

"I've never heard someone confess to a partial crime before Peter," the guy who looked like Brianna's dad spoke to the tall African-American man.

"Me either."

"So what's it going to be Christopher Hamilton?" Brianna's dad asked mildly. "Are you going to look for alternative employment forcibly or voluntarily?

Christopher looked at him. "You've got to be kidding me."

He looked around the room, but nobody was smiling. What were they? Some kind of mafia? They thought they could force people out of a job with these strong arm tactics? He'd show them. He'd call their bluff.

"You can't force me to leave. You've got nothing on me," he sneered.

"Dad," he motioned the oldest man in the room forward. The man had a small recording device in his hand. He flipped it on. Christopher listened in horror as his voice along with Shayla Thompson's spilled into the silence of the room. The words, the breathing, the expressions of ecstasy condemned him. That witch. She'd made copies!

"Turn it off dad," Brianna's father motioned to the older guy, a look of disgust on his face. "Now, we don't expect you back here tomorrow morning or any morning or any time after that. I don't care where you go as long as you're not near my daughter or my grandson. I think we understand each other, Mr. Hamilton. You can leave now."

The stocky guy opened the door, and Christopher Hamilton stumbled out on unsteady feet, his cockiness trumped by his evil doings. The harm he'd intended for Brianna had, like a boomerang, bounced back to him.

***

Outside, John Roach thanked each of his brothers and his dad for their support.

"How did you get this and so quickly?" his father asked, handing the recorder over to him.

"It helps to know people in the security and investigative business." He grinned. "There's a guy, Tony, who runs a personal security company called M.A.D. Nate actually told me about him. He helped me find Shayla Thompson. Christopher Hamilton had better watch out. She has a lot more copies of these based on what the M.A.D. investigator told me. She has the potential to become a blackmail nightmare for him."

"What he needs to do is quit running around and get to know the Lord for real," his dad said, opening his truck and climbing in. "I'll see you all on Sunday for your mom's surprise. He waved to his sons as he backed away.

"Remember, not a word to anyone about this. Bart and Bri are never to know," John warned as each man started out for his respective vehicle.

***

The next day during assembly at Grace Christian School, Mrs. Garner announced that due to a family crisis, Mr. Hamilton had to discontinue his employment with them. He had to return home to address the issue. There were murmurs of disappointment across the student body. He was such a nice man.

EPILOGUE

Brianna shot a look at her watch and stepped on the gas harder. She was more than an hour late for the surprise party for Mrs. Roach. Her mother and sisters-in-law had been blowing up her phone with calls and texts. Every one the same: *Bri, where are you?* She'd been off last week Sunday, so she worked this Sunday. Officially, the gym closed at six o'clock, but with paper work she always got out way after closing. To add to her lateness, the traffic going east into Long Island from Queens hadn't been easy. An accident had closed down the two left lanes at exit thirty-two and the back-up had been horrendous. She just cleared it. Brianna sighed. Oh, well, they'd just have to start without her. She had told Julia and the girls, the organizers of this event, that she might be late, although she hadn't anticipated running behind this much.

***

"Oh, thank God! You're finally here." Julia grabbed her and pulled her inside. Bri stumbled in, her hand still poised to ring the bell, which she hadn't gotten to do because her mother had flung open the front door and dragged her inside.

"Mom, what's the crisis? Didn't Mrs. Roach get here yet?"

Bri asked, looking at the slightly flustered chocolate version of herself.

"No. We delayed her because of you," Julia answered distractedly, pulling her towards the stairs. "You need to get changed. I thought you were coming dressed."

"I am dressed." Bri grinned, deliberately misunderstanding.

"I meant dressed up. This is a semi-formal event. Yoga pants and a t-shirt aren't going to work."

Brianna sniffed the air. The aromatic scents of basil blended with thyme and onions sharpened her hunger. "The food smells wonderful," she said, stepping into the guest bedroom at the top of the stairs. She hung the dress she brought on a hook behind the door, and started stripping down. "I've got to take a quick shower. I didn't have time at the gym."

"Oh, Bri, she's almost here!" her mother exclaimed in distress.

"Mom, then let them start without me. I can wish her happy birthday when I'm done, but I cannot go downstairs, smelling like sweat and deodorant breaking down."

Julia laughed at that, and Brianna rushed into the adjoining bathroom.

***

"You don't think it hugs my butt too much, mom?" Brianna asked, twisting to view her rear profile with a worried frown.

"Honey, you've got it so strut it is my policy."

Brianna laughed. Her mother had really emerged from her introverted shell since she married John who was not at all shy. She faced forward and smoothed her hands down the sides of the white lace dress she'd purchased a few weeks back. She and Tanya had been browsing online. The chic elegant lace cocktail dress had caught her eye. With its three quarter sleeves, Vneckline, and modest length—it stopped shy of her knees, Brianna hadn't been able to resist it. It came in black, pink, and white. She had wanted the pink but that was out of stock. She had another black cocktail dress so she chose the white one. It did look good on her though. She turned, admiring herself from all angles. While it did hug her closely in the rear, it was flattering and she felt good in it. For sure Bart would think so too. Brianna smiled as she thought about him. This marriage of theirs had been the real thing for a week now, and her only regret was that she had waited so long.

"Earth to Brianna."

She blinked and focused on her mother, standing to the side and waving a hand in her face. "Sorry I drifted a bit."

"I know honey. That happens when you're in love and being loved every night."

"Mom!" Brianna blushed.

Julia grinned. "Come. Let's fix your hair and then we can join the party."

"I'm not sure we can do anything with it. With all of the work outs I did today, I sweated every curl and wave out."

"That's fine. We're going for simple and elegant, not sophisticated and elaborate." She parted Brianna's hair slightly to the left, pulled her hair back a bit and secured it with a decorative hair comb. She brushed the other side forward a little so that it flowed down the right side of her daughter's face. "There, what do you think?"

Brianna looked at her reflection in the mirror. "Nice. Simple and elegant just like you said. Thanks mom." She stood up and hugged her mother.

Julia squeezed her hard and stepped back with a sniffle.

"What's the matter?" Bri asked, surprised.

"Nothing," Julia sniffed again, fanning her fingers before

her eyes, trying to get rid of the tears that way. "You're just so beautiful. My first born is independent, married, and all grown up. I'm so proud of you." She put a hand over her heart and fanned herself with the other in an attempt to compose herself.

"Oh, mommy," Brianna breathed, hugging Julia again. She didn't understand her mother's tears, but crying seemed contagious because she felt weepy herself.

"And," Julia went on when she caught her breath, "I'm so glad, you woke up and took hold of the local gold in your back yard. Bart is a good man, Bri. He's precious—gold like I said. I'm so glad you didn't let him slip through your fingers."

"Me too, mom. Me too."

Two sharp raps at the door got their attention. John's voice came through. "Julia, are you and Bri coming down? We're about to sing 'Happy Birthday' to mom."

Julia pulled herself together and answered her husband. "We're coming right now," she called, going to the door and opening it.

"Hey, pretty lady. Don't you look wonderful," her husband greeted her.

Julia rolled her eyes at Bri. "He's acting like he didn't see me earlier."

Brianna chuckled while she fastened the straps of her pink and white stilettos. Her mother complained, but she could hear the pleasure in her voice at her husband's compliment.

"It's just that you get more beautiful each time I see you," John grinned.

Julia made a face, but she kissed him. "Okay, let's go Bri," she said, taking her husband's arm and leaving the room.

***

Music wafted from the partially opened door of the living

119

room. Brianna figured it had to be either James or Mr. Roach playing the piano since John, the only other player in the family, was out here in the hallway.

"You first, pretty lady." John ushered his wife ahead of him, and she pushed the right side of the double door wider just as the left side started to swing open. "I've always wanted to do this, Bri," he said smiling down at his step-daughter.

"Do what?" she asked, glancing up at him with her brows knitted.

"This." He took her hand and placed it in the crook of his left arm.

What? Bri thought, swinging her gaze from him as the strains of the unchained melody filled the air. What in the world? Mr. and Mrs. Roach's living room had been converted into a giant nursery. There were flowers everywhere. The furniture wasn't where it usually was. In fact it wasn't anywhere in the room. Instead there were single chairs with what looked like pink silk covers lined up on either side of the room with bouquets of pink and white roses and carnations between them. Everybody was there—the entire Roach family. What was going on? And then she looked to the far left and started trembling. Lifting a badly shaking hand to her mouth, she gripped John's hand hard when everyone stood up and yelled, "Surprise!"

"J-John is this, is this…?"

"Your wedding," he finished with a smile. "Think you can stop shaking long enough to make it up the aisle?"

Tears running down her cheeks, she looked left again, and the man standing beneath the bridal arch smiling at her gave her the strength to reach him. John handed her over to her husband. As Brianna laid her hand on Bart's arm, she looked up at him with all the love she had for him displayed on her face. She cried, sniffled, and fanned like Julia had earlier in the room, trying to fan her tears away.

Bart offered her his handkerchief. "I thought you should have a wedding," he murmured. "Every couple needs memories, so I thought we would make some."

Dabbing her eyes, she choked, "You did all this?"

"I just gave the idea. The girls—your mom, Lauren, Stacy, and Pamela did all the work."

She would thank them later.

"Can we begin now?" Pastor Stafford, John and James' pastor who had been patiently standing there asked with a smile.

Brianna raised a finger. "Just a minute," she said. Turning to her husband, she did something that should have come a little later in the program. Slipping her arms around his neck, she touched her lips to his and kept that union going so long that the titters in the room changed to thunderous applause. When she pulled back, Bart looked like he wanted to keep at it. Pastor Stafford cut in and assured him he'd have all night for that and they should do the vows now. That had the audience as well as the bridal couple chuckling this time around.

***

They put Jonathon to bed together that night. Bart sat at Jon's beside and read their son a bed-time story while Brianna sat beside her husband and listened.

When Bart finished reading, the little boy yawned sleepily, and asked out of the blue, "Daddy, are you sleeping in mommy's bed again tonight?"

Brianna's face got warm. She'd wondered when he would get around to mentioning that. Bart had been sleeping in her bed for a week now.

"Yes, Jon, I am." Bart sounded amused.

"I'm glad," the little boy said. "But, mommy, doesn't daddy kick you at night anymore?"

Bart choked and Brianna glared at him. It was the story she had told Jon as an explanation of why she and Bart as husband and wife weren't sleeping together. Bart knew this so she didn't see why it was funny. "No, Jonathon, he doesn't," she answered their son.

"I got therapy," Bart volunteered his voice sounding quivery.

Brianna couldn't control a smile as she thought that indeed he'd gotten therapy. She had given him therapy every night in the past week. He'd been so exhausted he couldn't have kicked her off the bed even with an imaginary propensity to do so.

"What's therapy?" Jonathon asked.

"Something that you do over and over again to get rid of a problem," Brianna explained, tucking the comforter under his chin. "Now go to bed baby. You have school tomorrow." She leaned down and kissed him. His father did the same and turned out the light.

"Good night, daddy. G'night maaa," he mumbled, slurring his words as he drifted off.

Outside their son's room, Bart pulled his wife into his arms. "I've been thinking," he started, his hands doing a slow slide down her sides, "that I'm going to need some intensive therapy tonight."

Brianna unhooked his bowtie and started working on the buttons of his dress shirt. "Oh, you do," she said arching an interested eyebrow without breaking her task. "Because, I was thinking," she continued, pushing his shirt off his shoulders and letting her hands glide over his muscles, loving the feel of his strength beneath her palm, "of giving you some *explosive* therapy tonight."

"Whoa-hoa. Now that idea has me a hundred and ten percent on board."

"Do you want to know *how* I'm going to do it?" she asked suggestively, tucking her chin and giving him a sultry look from beneath her lashes.

"I'm all ears," he murmured, his lids going half mast as he gathered her snugly against his chest.

While she whispered, he acted, making a beeline for their room. If explosive therapy was anything like his wife was describing, Bart couldn't wait to experience it.

THE END

UPCOMING TITLES

A Matter of Trust
(Seneca Mountain Romances: Book 4)
<u>Coming July 2014</u>

Adrianna, Dri, wants to start a family. Her husband, Christopher, does too. Sounds like they're on the same page? Not quite. Haunted by an old tragedy, he wants to adopt. Dri wants to do things the traditional way. Christopher can't bring himself to give her what she wants. Reason, ranting, and rivers of tears don't change his mind. Dri hatches a private plan and secures his unwitting cooperation. But she doesn't remember that her condition can't be camouflaged forever. When her husband finds out what she has done, he is livid. With the trust between them torn down, Dri realizes too late that she got what she wanted at the expense of what she needs—her husband and his trust.

Emeralds Aren't Forever
(The Banning Island Romances: Book 3)
<u>Coming Fall 2014</u>

On a Spanish American Cruise vacation, Sarah has no idea how valuable the stone on her purse's clasp is. When she nearly gets mugged in Cartagena and almost thrown overboard later, she solicits help from the man who saved her both times— Everton Marsh. An ex-revolutionary and a sometimes security specialist, Everton had wanted a peaceful vacation. This American woman, Sarah, wasn't letting that happen. Together, they uncover a ring of emerald thieves, stretching from Cartagena to New York and to all parts of the Caribbean. Danger rises for Sarah as these thieves are willing to murder whoever blocks them from the emeralds. Now more than ever she needs Everton's protection. After a slow dance on a dark deck one night, Sarah realizes that she wants more than his protection.

EXISTING TITLES

Not His Choice
(Five Brothers' Books #4)
Excerpt

"The SAB stands for Second Advent Believers," she explained the acronym.

"I know."

"You're familiar with the denomination?"

"I would say so. I'm one of them."

Her eyes widened, and then her tiny lips split into a wide, pleasure-filled smile. "That's wonderful! Which conference are you with? Tri-State?"

The sliver of a smile that had been chasing the fringes of his mouth faded. She should have stopped at 'That's wonderful.' Although no one spoke about it, the SAB church still worshipped for the most part along racial lines—black and whites separately. The membership in Tri-State was predominantly black and in Northern mostly white. The fact that she concluded he was a Tri-State member because he was black said she thought stereotypically and worse still, it rang with racism.

"Wouldn't it be nice to stomp that stereotype out cold and throw that bigoted conclusion back in your face if I were to say I'm a member of your lily-white conference?"

Pamela could only sit and stare in shock at his scorn-laden words and the deep dislike in his eyes. Her thoughts tripped over themselves in reverse, trying to see what she'd said to set him off. Stereotype? Bigoted conclusion? Was he calling her a racist? For sure with the words 'lily-white' conference.

Shaken and at a loss for words, Pam scrambled in her vocabulary and found some to string together in a quivery statement. "I-I'm s-sorry, although I'm not sure what I'm apologizing for. Obviously, I offended you with something I said, and it wasn't my intent to do that."

He pushed his chair back and stood. Leveling a hostile look at her, he bit out, "It's never the intent of your people to offend; it's just inherent in your nature to do it." Giving her a killer look, he stalked away.

Your people? Pam's breath caught at the insult. Now who was being offensive? She stared at his departing back. Temper suddenly kicked her in the stomach, and then booted her in the rear end. She sailed off the seat in hot pursuit of that man, a mouthful of set-downs on the tip of her tongue.

Threading her way through the diners, she caught him just before he entered the kitchen. "Excuse me," she said, detaining him with a hand on his arm.

He stopped, sliced a carving-knife sharp look at her and dropped his gaze pointedly to her hand.

He deserved irritation. He'd made her mad. Why should she be the only one aggravated? Pam kept her hand in place and started talking. "You know nothing about me, so before you cast aspersions on my character, I suggest you find out who I am or keep your insults to yourself. First off, I'm no bigot. I've found that those quick to accuse others of prejudice are themselves prejudiced. Now, if I said something to offend you, be a man and tell me what it is instead of flying into a fit and being an ass."

Rage made your vision change colors. Peter hadn't believed it until this moment. Through a haze of red, battling an overwhelming desire to throttle the woman in front of him, he growled through his teeth. "TAKE. YOUR. HAND. OFF. MY. ARM."

Something in his face must have made her wise up, although she didn't look scared. She removed her hand.

They had an audience now. They hadn't been shouting, but anger had its unique octave and it attracted attention. The diners nearest to them watched with avid interest and open curiosity. Denny and two volunteers were hovering at the kitchen door. His look said *what in the name of all that's good is going on?* Peter ignored him. He had some final words for this woman. Leveling a glacial glare on Pamela Brinkley he hissed, "Let me make something clear to you, I'm a man and not an ass. Lucky for you, my mother raised me a gentleman. If not for that, you'd be flat on the floor, out cold." Raking a scathing look over her from head to toe, he shouldered his way past Denny and the others into the kitchen. He should have listened to the voice of caution and not approached that woman tonight. What a shrew!

Someone Like You
(Five Brothers' Books #3)
Excerpt

"I never asked you out!" She sounded appalled. Either she really was or was a pretender. He went with the latter since she was female.

"You implied that you wanted *me* to ask *you* out. Wasn't that the purpose of all that talk about my intentions towards you—that is, getting me to take you on a date?"

"You're delusional." Even as she said it, Stacy wasn't sure she believed it. Was that what she had subconsciously been trying to do? Despite his cynicism, downright down-on-women attitude, and outright rudeness sometimes, Nate Roach was interesting, and she did want to go out with him. There was just one thing to fix first. "You didn't do it right."

"Do what right?" His voice was wary like he thought she'd lost all cranial control.

"Ask me out properly," she told him.

"I don't know what's proper. I don't do this—dating, I mean. Truthfully, I don't want to do this. I just want my Bible back, and this seems like the best way to get it." Nate knew it wasn't true as soon as he said it. She fascinated him although he was fighting it. With her verve, she was an engaging conversationalist, a captivating phone companion. He had fun talking to her, sparring with her, and fielding her verbal volleys.

He felt alive, like he hadn't felt in years in female company. He wanted to see her. He just didn't want her to know what he really wanted.

"Okay," she was saying now, "I'll help you. Repeat after me, 'Stacy, will you go on a date with me tomorrow night?'"

"I will not," he growled uncooperatively.

Stacy sighed. "Obviously you're not a romantic. A gi—"

"*Obviously*," he interrupted in a *perish-the-thought* tone.

"A girl just likes to hear the words. It's nicer that way," she explained, her tone suggesting he was slow.

"I just want my Bible back."

"So you don't want to go on the date."

"That's a means to an end."

"Right. To get the Bible back." A coil of annoyance started in Stacy's abdomen. He could at least pretend to be interested. Suddenly, she didn't want to see him. She was interested, but not desperate. If he wasn't interested, why should she put herself and him through a date that would be a trial for both of them? "You know what, Nate, come to Queens to get the Bible. I don't want to go out with you. Is this your cell?"

"Yes," he said slowly, like he was unsure whether he was coming or going.

"Good. I'll text my address to you. Good night."

Nate looked angrily at his iPhone's screen. Why did women have to be so contrary, complicated, and downright difficult? He swore they did it on purpose. He was very offended that after putting words into his mouth to invite her out, she'd refused when he did. She had sounded miffed too. He wondered what had upset *her*. He hadn't said a thing that he could think of. His phone beeped. It was a text message with her address. She lived in Rosedale. She had the nerve to tell him to come at seven o'clock sharp tomorrow evening. Nate decided to watch the news instead of going to bed. He was too irritated.

Once in This Lifetime
(Five Brothers' Books #2)
Excerpt

So here she was on a plane on this early Monday morning with John in the middle of the row, between her and Bri. He was asleep. He'd asked the flight attendant for a pillow and had promptly propped it on Julia's shoulder, settled himself comfortably, and drifted into la-la land. Bri was watching a movie, her head phones in her ears. Julia had a novel, but she didn't feel like reading right now. John's hand had slipped from the arm rest to her thigh and was resting with increasing pressure, warmth, and stimulation as his sleep deepened. She brushed her knuckles over his jaw lightly and the shadow of bristles scratched her hand. He hadn't shaved this morning. His four o'clock shadow gave him a ruggedly handsome appearance. In repose, he looked relaxed and younger than his thirty-six years. His lips kept calling her attention, but she kept resisting, knowing if her gaze lingered on his mouth too long she would kiss him. She didn't want to do that in front of Bri and everyone else. Helplessly she traced the bridge of his straight nose with her forefinger and followed the line of his lips around his mouth. He was a gorgeous man, inside and outside. The more she looked at him, the more tender her feelings for him grew. He was a patient man, one with endurance—longsuffering—but he could be pushed over the edge as he had been yesterday. Julia knew she couldn't take him for granted. He was a kind man, a caring person, sociable, warm, and loving...extremely loving. He made her feel so special and fragile and delicate and unique with his attention, his kisses, his endearments, and his caresses. Watching him, Julia realized he wasn't a man she could let go. Her heart communicated the thought clearly, and right on its heels, the knowledge came that she was in love with John Roach. Julia closed her eyes as the awareness washed over her. It wasn't somewhere that she had intended to go, but it had happened. The question was, did she want to do something about it? Besides, how did he feel about her? Did he love her?

Slipping her hand beneath his palm on her thigh she intertwined their fingers, needing the intimate contact with the love now pulsing in her heart for him. Her eyes flew back to his face when he returned the pressure of her fingers against his. Brilliant blue eyes, wide open, met hers. With a lazy smile curling up the corners of his mouth he greeted her, "How's my pretty lady?"

Julia smiled at him and thought, your pretty lady is loving you privately like crazy. Aloud she declared her intention prior to action. "Wanting to kiss you," she whispered and proceeded to do that, despite Bri and the passengers across the aisle.

From Passion to Pleasure
(Five Brothers' Books #1)
Excerpt

"No, I'm not going," she objected emphatically.

"Excuse me?" He sounded like he didn't think his hearing was reliable.

"I'm not going to the caterer with you tomorrow to change the menu," she told him clearly. "And I don't appreciate your high-handedness in dictating to me that I have to go."

"My high-handedness?" He sounded incredulous. "I never dictated anything. I clearly and deliberately used the word *suggest.*"

At the moment Lauren couldn't remember what word he'd used and being in no mood to exercise her brain in recollection, she didn't even try. She was too upset and too tired and too emotional and undoubtedly tomorrow she would regret all. However, right now she wanted this man to get it into his head that he couldn't boss her around, and her opinions and feelings counted, and she would make them heard! She proceeded to do just that. "James, I told you I have a very strong objection to serving meat at the wedding, and I feel that you should consider my concerns and respect them. Frankly I feel like you're trying to railroad me into doing what I don't want to do."

"So this is all about you, is it?" The question was heated, like his control on his temper was slipping. "I don't have any input. My wishes are irrelevant. I thought for a marriage to happen two people, male and female, had to be involved. Obviously you've redefined marriage to a solitary state. In short, you've cut me out of the picture. Maybe I should take you seriously and stay out of the picture."

Fear and fury clutched simultaneously at Lauren's throat and chest, restricting her air supply and making her heart thunder like train wheels clattering over railroad tracks. Was he trying to break their engagement? The question floated fleetingly as fury rose higher; and like a Tsunami roaring in from the depths of the ocean to the shore, it exploded into a raging torrent of words that Lauren would later wish she hadn't said. Her voice shaking with the depth of her anger, she shouted, "Maybe you should! Maybe this marriage is too premature. Maybe we're not suited at all. Right now I'm no longer sure I even want to marry someone as controlling as you!"

The silence that followed her outburst was thunderous. When James finally spoke his tone was deadly calm and rang with coldness. "Maybe you're not the only one unsure of this marriage, and maybe you are right. You shouldn't marry me. Good night, Lauren."

All Things Work Together
(Seneca Mountain Romances #3)
Excerpt

"I want to talk to you about Adam."

Jasmine's spine stiffened. She knew where this wind was blowing. "What about him?" she asked calmly.

He sat back in his office chair and folded his arms across his chest. "He told me that you confiscated his phone last night."

"Did he tell you why?" Jasmine raised her eyebrows, the question flavored a bit with spunk.

"He was on it after curfew, but th—"

"For the third night in a row," she interrupted, emphasizing the magnitude of the misdeed.

"Yes, I know all that, but that's not the part I have a problem with."

"Oh?" There were parts to this now? And why would he have a problem? Hadn't he been concerned about her maintaining order in his household? Now he had a problem when she fulfilled his wishes?

"When Adam got his phone back there were three international calls made from it. Two to Jamaica and one to St. Thomas."

Jasmine sat statue-still in her chair, hearing the accusation he hadn't articulated. She raised a forefinger, "Wait one minute. If there were international calls on his phone, I didn't make them."

"The times of the calls were when you had the phone in your possession," he pointed out.

He still hadn't accused her outright, but he didn't have to. He believed she made those calls. That was clearer than day. Adam King, Jr. was a crafty boy. She hadn't expected this. Jasmine wouldn't underestimate him again, but if he thought he could intimidate her into not enforcing the rules his dad put in place, he'd better think twice. But first things first. One problem at a time. "Look, Pastor King, I just told you I did not make those calls. Obviously you don't believe me. The fact that you've persisted with the issue by pointing out that I had the phone at the times of the calls, implying that no other person could have made the calls, tells me that you'll believe your son's word over mine. I understand that. I'm a stranger still, and he's your child. However, you might want to consider a couple of things: I have my own phone. Why would I use your son's? The day we met, you doubted whether I understood teenagers or whether I could care for them. At the risk of being insubordinate, I'm now wondering how much *you* understand teenagers?"

He leaned forward in his chair, his expression hard. The chill in his eyes said her words had struck a chord. Jasmine wasn't trying to get fired, but she'd learned it's best to start as you mean to go on. Don't take things docilely, especially when you're not at fault. Be firm, frank, and as much as possible be polite, but speak your mind.

"Have you considered that Adam was the one who made those calls?" she asked.

"Why would he do that?" His tone could turn a water droplet to an icicle.

"Because he was angry that I took his phone, he wanted to get back at me. He probably hoped to intimidate me into not doing it again if he got me in trouble with you."

"You don't know my children like I do, Ms. Lewis. Adam isn't the kind of child to be cunning like that," he objected.

"Sometimes I wonder if you know your children at all, Pastor." Okay she was having a problem with the 'be polite' part. Now the words were out, and she could not take them back. Jasmine didn't try to fix it because she couldn't.

"What's that supposed to mean?" His eyebrows went south and his mouth firmed into a displeased line, annoyance shadowing his expression like storm clouds darkening the skies.

"You work all the time. They don't see you. Do you know that Claire wishes you worked fewer hours so you could spend more time with her? Do you know that Adam sleeps restlessly some nights and cries out for you?" She watched surprise and hurt do a fast exchange in his expression before he camouflaged it. "And do you know that he also cries out for his mother?"

"Enough!" The word struck like thunder, cracking the air like lightning.

Jasmine jerked and watched pain and anger perform a visible struggle in his face. He inhaled a significant portion of the oxygen in the air and exhaled slowly. "I might not know everything there is to know about my kids," he started, his voice tight and his words measured. "And maybe I do need to spend time with them," he continued through his teeth. "But you don't know them period. You don't know any of us. You have no idea what we've been through as a family, what we still go through. Do me a favor and clear it with me before you punish my kids and please don't ever mention their mother again. Goodnight, Ms. Lewis." With that he left his chair and opened the door.

Stunned, she sat there for some moments before grasping that this was a dismissal. She rose slowly and approached the door with even more lethargic steps. At the door she paused, not sure what to say, but feeling compelled to make an exit statement. She looked up at him, but he was staring determinedly at some point beyond her, his jaw like granite. Jasmine wet her lips. "I'm sorry. I didn't mean to stir up old hurts. I was just trying to—"

"Good. Night. Ms. Lewis." The words came out with forceful pace, the emotion in them bordering on violence.

Jasmine sailed out the door. She knew when she had overstayed her welcome.

A Price Too High
(Seneca Mountain Romances #2)
Excerpt

As it turned out, he was speechless when he opened the door and saw her, but then so was she. The sight of him in a ridged undershirt that outlined every muscle on his chest and showcased his powerful biceps tumbled her thoughts into a steamy memory of tangled sheets, urgent kisses, frenzied caresses, and the mind-blowing passion that they had shared on their sole night together.

He was staring at her stomach like it was a UFO and this was his very first time seeing one. If their roles were reversed, maybe she would be shocked too. Karen passed her tongue over her lips and forced herself to speak. "Hi, Douglas. May I come in?"

Shock sped away fast. His eyes jumped from her belly to her face and the fury blazing in his gaze made Karen cringe. "You lying, scheming, wicked user!" Every vitriolic word barreled through his clenched teeth and slammed Karen like assault weapons' firepower, each hit leaving her fighting for breath and struggling to stay on her feet with the unmasked hatred in them. His voice rising, he accused, "You *left* me on our wedding night, skulking away like a thief without having the decency or courage to tell me to my face how you truly felt about my family and why you had really married me. You sent me an inadequate text message after you fled, leaving me reeling and wondering how you could say you love me, how you could make love with me and then use me as a vessel for revenge. You never returned my numerous calls and then you disconnected your phone. Now seven months later you show up at my door and expect *me* to let *you* in?"

Tears, hot and stinging pooled in her eyes, and her throat ached with the effort not to cry out at the scorn and disdain in her husband's face. She hadn't expected a positive reception, but neither had she been prepared for the magnitude of his venom. By force of will alone, she managed to keep her tears at bay, but her voice still wobbled when she spoke. "I-I n-need to talk to you, Doug. P-please let me in."

He looked at her for a long time, the repugnance in his expression unchanged, before he turned and walked back into the apartment, leaving the door open. Karen bit her lip, thinking that the open door meant she could enter. She crossed the threshold with cautious steps.

A Fall for Grace
(Seneca Mountain Romances #1)
Excerpt

"Solomon, this isn't going to work. I can't—."

"Shh," he said, silencing her negatives and pessimism with a finger against her lips. "I love you," he declared and then repeated it, enunciating the words so there would be no incomprehension, "*I love you*. And I'm not going to let you throw what we have and all we can have away. The Bible tells us to ask, seek, and knock and doors will open for us. I am going to keep asking, seeking, and knocking until you open your heart to me. I'm going to be like that widow who the judge got tired of and just gave her what she wanted. You're the judge. Consider me the petitioner. I'm not going to stop telling you that I love you, that I need you, that I refuse to live my life any more without you until you get tired, surrender and give me what we both want and need."

Looking into his eyes, Grace was captivated by the determination in those dark depths. The intensity of his speech and the sincerity of his words were breaking through the invisible walls of resistance that she'd erected. If he kept at it tonight, she wasn't sure she'd last with this battle against the onslaught of his love. Could she really take a chance on him? Should she take a chance on him? Would she have regrets later if she let him go? If she yielded to the pull and poignancy of this moment, and accepted the love he'd declared, received the permanence with him that he was offering, would she have regrets later?

He pulled her into his arms, letting her feel the hardness of him against her tender places, stirring desire in her heart and in places that should stay asleep until wedded bliss. He kissed the corner of her mouth. "Take a chance on me Grace," he coaxed, his voice a seductively husky sound. It was like he'd read her mind. She felt the foundations of her fortress give way and begin crumbling. "You won't regret it," he promised and whatever barriers she'd set up against him buckled under the weight of his persistence. "I love you, Grace." In her heart, she whispered the same. Aloud she promised to take a chance on him for the second time that week.

ABOUT THE AUTHOR

A believer in happy endings and forever after type stories, Brigette has been an avid romance reader since her teens. Inspired by her own real life romance with her husband, Clifford, she began writing romance novels after the birth of her first child and hasn't stopped since. Brigette holds a degree in Cultural Studies with a concentration in communication. She lives in the northeastern U.S.A. with her husband and four children. She can be reached at hearthavenbooks@gmail.com or visit www.brigettemanie.com. Other places to reach Brigette are…

https://www.amazon.com/Brigette-Manie/e/B00A3CPJC4

https://www.goodreads.com/author/show/6562932.Brigette_Manie

https://www.facebook.com/brigette.manie.author?ref=stream

https://twitter.com/BrigetteManie

CPSIA information can be obtained at www.ICGtesting.com
Printed in the USA
LVOW06s2138260715

447744LV00008B/116/P